HAMLET

A New Version

SHAKESPEARE'S

HAMLET

A New Version by

ROUBEN
MAMOULIAN

THE BOBBS-MERRILL COMPANY, INC.
PUBLISHERS

A Subsidiary of HOWARD W. SAMS & CO., INC.

INDIANAPOLIS · NEW YORK · KANSAS CITY

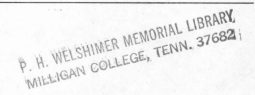

P. H. WELSHIMER MEMORIAL LIBRARY
MILLIGAN COLLEGE, TENN. 37682

PR
2807
.A2
M293

Professionals and amateurs are hereby warned that SHAKESPEARE'S HAMLET being fully protected under the copyright laws of the United States of America, the British Empire including the Dominion of Canada, and all other countries of the Universal Copyright and Berne Conventions, is subject to royalty. All rights including professional, amateur, motion picture, recitation, lecturing, public reading, radio and television broadcasting, and the rights of translation into foreign languages are strictly reserved. Particular emphasis is laid on the question of reading, permission for which must be secured from the author's agent in writing. All inquiries for amateur and stock productions should be addressed to The Bobbs-Merrill Company, Inc., 3 West 57th Street, New York, New York 10019. Inquiries for all other rights should be addressed to Paul R. Reynolds, Inc., 599 Fifth Avenue, New York, New York 10017.

First Printing, 1965
Copyright © 1965 by Rouben Mamoulian
All Rights Reserved
Library of Congress Catalog Card Number 65-26510

PRINTED IN THE UNITED STATES OF AMERICA

Contents

42375

FOREWORD

The text of *Hamlet*, which has remained virtually unchanged for three and one-half centuries, is here revised.

I feel that a "decent respect to the opinions of mankind requires" that I declare the causes which impelled me to do this, and I hope that after I have done so, you will be convinced that I was motivated not by reckless presumption but by the most humble and fervent admiration for *Hamlet* and its author.

First. The original text of *Hamlet* not only has become obscure and hard to understand, but, in many instances, invites misapprehensions.

Second. An incredible amount of nonsense has been written about the play, not only by amateurs and mischief-makers but also by a number of respected writers, Shakespearean scholars and critics.

Third. The first two causes have succeeded to an appalling degree in confusing and misleading the readers of *Hamlet* and, even more important, bringing about woeful distortions of Shakespeare's masterwork in most of its recent theatrical productions.

In revising the text of *Hamlet* my object was not to change Shakespeare—only a fool would want to do that—but to make him fully intelligible to the present-day reader and spectator. His power and glory and the rhythm of his verse remain inviolate, while the true meaning of his words and phrases is, I hope, made clearer.

For over 360 years, while *Hamlet* was being published in its original form, the English language has been undergoing constant and drastic changes. A great many words have become archaic and obsolete, and a vast number, while still in usage in current English, have changed their meanings.

For example, let me mention just a few words at random from *Hamlet* which have ceased to be part of modern English: (1) bisson, (2) bodkin, (3) cautel, (4) cote, (5) crants, (6) gules, (7) imposthume, (8) statist, (9) meed, (10) milch, (11) overpeer, (12) reechy, (13) cataplasm, (14) cess. These words meant: (1) blinding, (2) dagger, (3) deceit, (4) pass by, (5) garlands, (6) red, (7) abscess, (8) statesman, (9) wages, (10) moist, (11) tower above, (12) filthy, (13) plaster, (14) cessation.

Surely few readers today would understand these words unless they were expert in Elizabethan English. They would also misunderstand a multitude of words which, though still a part of our language, have radically changed their meaning. Again, for example (what these words actually meant when Shakespeare wrote them in *Hamlet* follows in parentheses): aim (guess), antic (odd, fantastic), idle (mad, crazy), still (always), by and by (immediately), cousin (nephew), ecstasy (madness), front (brow), general (the public, the common people), capable (sensitive), jump (just), let (hinder), luxury (lust), rival (partner), thrift (profit), woundless (invulnerable), valanced (bearded).

Because of the profusion of such words it has become necessary during the last hundred years or so for most editions of *Hamlet* to carry long glossaries to the play. These have grown more and more voluminous with each edition, until the publications of *Hamlet* carry glossaries and appendixes as thick as the play itself.

In addition to these now-obscure words there are numerous expressions throughout the text which, though undoubtedly clear to the spectators at the Globe, have by now also lost their meanings. In many cases even their origins cannot be traced with absolute certainty. This brings forth a further mass of footnotes to the text.

Thus the reading of *Hamlet*, instead of being the lusty, exalted pleasure it should be, has become a tiring task of study and research, with the reader's attention distracted with every other line to either the footnote or the glossary. It ceases to be a joy and becomes a labor, certainly to the average reader.

No one likes to read something he cannot understand. The purpose of language is communication. When words cease to communicate meanings, they are dead; and when they convey meanings unintended by the author, they are treacherous. Why then should they be left in the text of the most viable play—*Hamlet*—by the most gloriously alive author—Shakespeare?

I think the reason no Shakespearean play has ever been revised to conform with contemporary English is largely due to the excessive veneration in which the author is held. I am sure that in some quarters the attempt to revise any of Shakespeare's words or rewrite any of his lines would be considered a sacrilege. I submit that this kind of veneration is misdirected. This is to "love not wisely, but too well."

It reminds me of a legend (which does not exist, but ought to) about the Japanese peasant who saw that his Emperor had fallen into a pit during a hunt and was lying there with a broken leg, unable to move. Now, the peasant could have easily gotten him out and saved him, but he worshiped his Emperor and did not dare to break the sacred law which forbade him to touch the divine person of His Majesty. So the peasant sat at the edge of the pit and watched his monarch languish in misery and pain.

We have been watching Shakespeare's *Hamlet*, as well as his other plays, gradually recede further and further from the grasp of the average reader because of the language pit. All attempts to cure this through the medium of interminable footnotes and glossaries are futile. They are well-intentioned but stifling, for they make of a great artistic creation, designed for direct understanding and spontaneous enjoyment, a textbook, a scientific exercise, requiring detailed research and study.

It is indeed a proof of Shakespeare's transcendent genius that, in spite of all this, he still is one of the most active powers in the artistic life of mankind. Even now, in a world cruelly split into hostile camps, he retains his throne and sceptre in every land.

But let us face some other sober facts about Shakespeare's position today, especially in English-speaking countries. Right and left, one hears how great he is, how much he is read, how frequently performed, how intimately known to every man, woman, and child; how admired, how loved! I submit that this is not all true. This may apply to a limited group of writers, intellectuals, and bibliophiles (though even here there are many notable exceptions), but with the overwhelming majority it is but a façade, a sadly pretentious and pathetic hypocrisy. To them Shakespeare is not the great spiritual gift-bearer, not even a creative idea, but merely a slogan. Our modern life is stuffed with slogans and shibboleths, and Shakespeare has become one of them; at best a status symbol, a kind of famous museum piece, heard about and talked about by many, enjoyed and understood by few. The truth is, they have not read him, or they cannot read him. They have collided with him once—in high school or college, perhaps—when some of his incomprehensible lines were stuffed down unwilling throats. Many have never overcome this traumatic experience. Some will tell you that they have attempted to renew the acquaintance in their more mature years, but the bitter taste of memories lingered, and the obscurities of language remained as dense and discouraging as ever. I think Shakespeare deserves better than that.

Why allow the metamorphosis of the English language to obscure and dull the impact of a play as modern, meaningful, and exciting as *Hamlet*?

Shakespeare, unique in many ways, is also a paradox in literature: Here is the greatest English writer, whose language is clearly understood, word by word, by every foreign nation in the world—but not by English-speaking people! His plays have been translated into seventy-nine foreign languages, translated into contemporary, living idiom, not their sixteenth- or seventeenth-century forms. Thus every word is clear to a foreigner. This, regardless of whether the translation is good or bad.

My own first personal contact with Shakespeare took place when I was a schoolboy. I saw *Hamlet* performed, then read it in Armenian, in Russian, and in French; and I understood every word. When I began to learn English, the greatest thrill I looked forward to was to read him in the original. This I did, but with a shocking result: I couldn't understand half of it. At first I attributed this to my insufficient knowledge of English. Later, when my English improved enough for me to enjoy and understand other great writers in English, I found that I still could not understand many of Shakespeare's words and expressions.

My love for Shakespeare was too active and vital to let it go at that. So I buried myself in stacks of glossaries, dictionaries, footnotes, appendixes, and all sorts of research material. It took me a long time before I could honestly feel that I knew what every line in *Hamlet* meant, at least in terms of language. With this knowledge my appreciation of *Hamlet* increased a hundredfold. So much of its meaning, its wisdom and beauty, its complete "rightness," had been hidden from me before. Now it unfolded in all its iridescent glory. And then I thought, what a tragic loss it is for millions of English-speaking people, young and old, not to be able to read *Hamlet* the way they can read any contemporary book or most of the great classics—intelligently and fluently, without being constantly stopped by the cumbersome mechanics of language. The several years, on and off, during which I occupied myself with *Hamlet* were well worth it to me. More, working on it was one of the most exciting adventures of my life. But it is neither fair nor necessary to expect every reader to expend that much time and effort in order to enjoy *Hamlet* fully. Why not let him benefit, in the easiest and most direct manner, by the philological research already done by many dedicated scholars? Why not go an important step farther—revise the text itself, replace all its archaisms and obscurities with words and expressions of modern, living English? Why not make it spontaneously intelligible to the present-day reader and spare him the irksome, joy-killing necessity of constantly consulting footnotes, glossaries, and appendixes? This latter procedure would be deadening enough with a work in prose—with dramatic poetry, and especially Shakespeare's poetry, which flows like a Niagara, it is fatal. Why shouldn't the supreme masterpiece of the greatest English writer be as accessible to the understanding of those who speak his own tongue as it is to Germans, Frenchmen, Russians, Armenians, and other foreigners? In short, I felt that what *Hamlet* needed was a good English translation.

Some things in life seem unthinkable until someone does them. Once done—after a possible initial shock and, perhaps, a

few outraged cries of "Heresy!"—they are found to be bene-
ficial and welcome. And then everybody wonders why this
particular thing had not been realized long before, for it now
appears to have been obviously needed and, in fact, inevitable.

For many years I had hoped—and even more, felt sure—
that any bright day would bring the publication of a revised
Hamlet that could be freely read, understood, and relished not
only by the small circle of Shakespearean experts but also by
the great mass of average readers who have heretofore been
deprived of this tremendous and joyful experience. When this
did not happen, I decided to do it myself.

I worked on it with a constant sense of heavy responsi-
bility. Modifying Shakespeare is a frightening occupation.
What kept me going was the conviction that what I was doing
was right and needed, that it was both a tribute and a service
to a great master without whom life would be considerably
duller.

HAMLET REVISED

THE REVISIONS I have made in the text of *Hamlet* comprise the
following:

About 2000 words replaced by their modern equivalents.
About 100 lines rewritten.
About 510 lines eliminated.
Changing the spelling of some words throughout the play.
*Rearranging most of the words which had to be read as bi-
syllables so that they can now be read in the usual manner,
and accenting with diacritical marks the few that are still
to be read as such.*
Revising punctuation.
Dividing the play into four Acts, instead of five.
Indicating the time intervals between Scenes and Acts.

Determining Hamlet's age as twenty, instead of thirty.
Specifying the probable ages of other characters in the
play.
Turning some asides into dialogue.
Eliminating some of the "traditional" actions in the play.
And, lastly, writing stage directions into the play.

WORDS REPLACED / The reason for changing a multitude of words in the text I have already explained. It is obvious that you cannot fully enjoy reading a play or pass any kind of judgment upon it unless, first, you understand the words—this certainly is the bare minimum requirement. Even with this prerequisite, a play is more difficult to read than any other form of literature.

Let me give just a couple of examples of how misleading to the proper understanding of *Hamlet* some of the archaisms are.

In Act I, Scene 4, the Ghost repeatedly beckons Hamlet to follow him. Horatio and Marcellus urge Hamlet against it, and finally try to restrain him physically, by holding him back.

HAMLET

Still am I called, unhand me, gentlemen . . .
By heaven, I'll make a ghost of him that *lets* me!
I say, away! . . .

(The italics are mine.)

To us, the meaning of that second line is garbled. "Him that lets me" stands for something quite different today. In Shakespeare's time the word let meant "hinder." So I revised the line to read:

By heaven, I'll make a ghost of him that *holds* me.

Another example, and a much more important one. After "the play-within-the-play," when Hamlet has finally forced the King into a silent confession of his crime, Rosencrantz and Guildenstern enter to tell Hamlet that the Queen, his mother, desires to speak to him in her room. While Hamlet is still talking to them, Polonius enters.

POLONIUS

My lord, the queen would speak with you, and *presently*.

And after a few lines:

HAMLET

Then I will come to my mother *by and by*.
. . . I will come *by and by*.

POLONIUS

I will say so.

HAMLET

"*By and by*" is easily said.—Leave me friends.

(ACT III, SCENE 2)

(Again the italics are mine.)

Now, the word *presently* used by Polonius meant "at once"; and *by and by*, three times uttered by Hamlet, meant "immediately." You can see how necessary it is to replace them with their modern equivalents in order to understand the true impact of this passage. Hamlet's repetition of *by and by* and his last " 'By and by' is easily said" are utterly meaningless. But replace them with *immediately*, and you will see a dramatic point of utmost importance being advisedly made by Shakespeare. This thrice-emphasized "immediately" relates to the very core of the tragedy: Hamlet's alleged procrastination, which virtually all critics consider to be the main "problem" of the play. For more than a hundred years they have been asking: Why does not Hamlet avenge his father immediately? And for just as long Hamlet has been replying: " 'Immediately' is easily said." But this keeps falling on deaf ears.

[11]

My choice of which words to change was helped by imagining what William Shakespeare would do if he were still living today (and I wish to heaven he were). I'm sure that, noting the transformations which have taken place in the English language since he "shuffled off this mortal coil," the first thing he would do would be to make certain that every word properly expressed what he meant 363 years ago. He would not want *Hamlet*, a play more modern than any written at present, to sound archaic. To help it further he would replace all the "*thou's*" and verbs connected with them with "*you's*" and modern tenses of the verbs.

This I have tried to do.

In regard to "*thou's*," I left them intact in the two encounters between the Ghost and Hamlet (Act I, Scene 5 and Act III, Scene 4), because in these they contribute majestically to the grand structure and sonorous music of Shakespeare's verse. Here Shakespeare truly creates with words a marble monument. To replace "*thou's*" with "*you's*" here would turn marble into soft wood.

Listen to this:

GHOST

I could a tale unfold whose lightest word
Would harrow up thy soul, freeze thy young blood,
Make thy two eyes, like stars, start from their spheres . . .

(ACT I, SCENE 5)

Now, hear how it pales with "*you's*":

I could a tale unfold whose lightest word
Would harrow up your soul, freeze your young blood,
Make your two eyes, like stars, start from their spheres . . .

And this:

[12]

Hamlet

>   . . . Remember thee?
> Ay, thou poor ghost, while memory holds a seat
> In this distracted globe. Remember thee? . . .
>
>   (ACT I, SCENE 5)

Now, hear how much power it would lose with "*you's*":

>   . . . Remember you?
> Yes, you poor ghost, while memory holds a seat
> In this distracted globe. Remember you? . . .

In replacing the archaic words with their present-day equivalents, the main difficulty lay in preserving at the same time the rhythm and spirit of Shakespeare's verse. The task would have been much easier were the play written in prose. I never allowed myself to disturb its iambic structure. This caused me, at times, to spend long, agonizing hours in search of a word, or a line, which would convey the proper meaning, yet keep the rhythm intact.

LINES REWRITTEN / There are many passages in *Hamlet*, some quite long, which contain so many obsolete and misleading words, and a syntax so archaic and confusing, that I felt it necessary to rephrase them, as well as condense them in some instances. In doing this I tried my best to keep up to the style of the original.

Here are a few examples:

Horatio

>   . . . now sir, young Fortinbras
> Of únimpróvéd mettle hot and full,
> Hath in the skirts of Norway here and there
> Sharked up a list of lawless résolútes

[13]

For food and diet to some enterprise
That hath a stomach in't, which is no other,
As it doth well appear unto our state,
But to recover of us by strong hand
And terms compulsatory, those foresaid lands
So by his father lost; . . .

(ACT I, SCENE I)

I have rephrased this into:

> . . . Now, sir, young Fortinbras,
> Of yet untempered mettle hot and full,
> Has in the skirts of Norway here and there
> Picked up a band of idle, lawless cutthroats—
> This, to recover from us by strong hand
> Those foresaid lands so by his father lost; . . .

Another passage:

FIRST PLAYER

But who, O, who had seen the mobled queen
Run barefoot up and down, threat'ning the flames
With bisson rheum; a clout upon that head
Where late the diadem stood, and for a robe,
About her lank and all o'erteeméd loins,
A blanket, in the alarm of fear caught up;
Who this had seen, with tongue in venom steeped
'Gainst Fortune's state would treason have pronounced.
But if the gods themselves did see her then,
When she saw Pyrrhus make malicious sport
In mincing with his sword her husband's limbs,
The instant burst of clamor that she made—
Unless things mortal move them not at all—

[14]

Would have made milch the burning eyes of heaven
And passion in the gods.

(ACT II, SCENE 2)

Now this reads:

But who, O, who had seen the muffled queen
Run barefoot up and down, threatening the flames
With blinding tears; a rag upon that head
Where late the diadem stood; and for a robe,
A blanket, in the alarm of fear caught up—
Who this had seen, with tongue in venom steeped
Would have rebelled 'gainst Fortune's cruel power.
But if the gods themselves did see her then,
When she saw Pyrrhus make malicious sport
In mincing with his sword her husband's limbs,
The instant burst of clamour that she made—
Unless things mortal move them not at all—
Would have made weep the burning eyes of heaven,
And stirred the gods to passion!

Another passage:

HAMLET

    . . . O such a deed
As from the body of contraction plucks
The very soul, and sweet religion makes
A rhapsody of words; heaven's face does glow,
And this solidi´ty and compound mass
With heated visage, as against the doom,
Is thought-sick at the act.

(ACT III, SCENE 4)

This now reads:

> . . . O, such a deed
> As from the holy rite of wedding plucks
> The very soul, and sweet religion makes
> A noise of empty words! Heaven's face does blush,
> And this great mass, this solid globe of earth,
> With gloom-struck visage, as if doomsday's here,
> Is thought-sick at the act.

CUTS IN THE TEXT / Making cuts in *Hamlet* is a dangerous and risky operation. One must remind oneself, constantly, that Shakespeare was a genius, the greatest of playwrights, and that he knew every moment what he was doing and why.

It has almost become a pernicious fashion for many critics, stumped by certain passages in *Hamlet* and unable to unravel their correct meaning, to put the blame on Shakespeare —on his thoughtlessness, his hasty, casual writing, his slipshod borrowing from older sources of elements unfitting to his conception. This, of course, is as ridiculous as it is arrogant. The fault is with the critic's own lack of art and perception.

Because of the unmatched lifelike complexity, richness, and subtlety of Shakespeare's writing, it is very easy to pass a hurried and foolish judgment upon a scene or a passage and decide that their deletion would improve the play. I must confess this has happened to me, too. I found it very easy to make cuts in *Hamlet* before I fully realized what *Hamlet* was. The better I came to know the play, the more difficult it became to cut it. Many a time a cut I had made, and not necessarily a big one, would haunt and bother me for days, until finally, and fortunately, my brain would awaken from its stupor and discover how important that passage was, how vitally and marvelously necessary to the scheme of the play. I realized that the trouble was not with Shakespeare, but with my own inability spontaneously to perceive the deeper facets of Shakespeare's grand design. I had learned the folly of underrating Shakespeare's skill. This taught me to proceed most cautiously and most humbly with any cuts. Thus, every cut in the text was made only after a long and soul-searching deliberation—my conscience stood strict watch over my shoulder.

I don't believe I have eliminated anything that contributes materially to either the progress of the play or the fullness of its texture and its characters. I used a careful scalpel, and only on lines and segments variously concerned with items which were of topical interest to Shakespeare's audience, but for us have little or no meaning; elaborations of points already fully made; passages which seem unnecessarily to clutter the action and impede its flow; phrases used only because the mechanics of the Elizabethan uncurtained and sceneryless stage required them (and I am sure Shakespeare put them in reluctantly, as an unavoidable necessity). In brief, I think I can "answer well" for every cut I made.

Hamlet is the longest of all Shakespeare's plays, and, by our present standards of theatrical productions, overlong in performance. Although in its time it kept in constant grip even the "groundlings," who had to stand on their feet for hours, it proves fatiguing to our pampered contemporary audiences (or, perhaps, standing is less painful than being squeezed into our narrow, knee-breaking, real estate-saving theatre seats). So, with very rare exceptions, *Hamlet*, when performed, is cruelly cut. There would be nothing wrong with some cutting, done within reason. The trouble and the mischief is that almost all directors, or actors, hack out many of the play's most vital and essential scenes and passages. They do it with reckless and foolhardy abandon.

May I note here that the deletions I made in this version

[17]

are for the *readers* of *Hamlet*. For the *spectators*, who are seeing *Hamlet* performed on the stage, a few more cuts would be possible, cuts which will not affect the vital tissues of the play or its broad scope. These cuts would be compensated for by the actors' performances. Good acting and proper stage direction can make certain lines and passages in a play expendable. But the reader needs them, because he has only the written words to follow, and not live, flesh-and-blood action on the stage.

Here are some examples of cuts and condensations.

The following is part of the conversation between Hamlet, Rosencrantz, and Guildenstern referring to the traveling Players:

HAMLET

. . . What players are they?

ROSENCRANTZ

Even those you were wont to take such delight in, the tragedians of the city.

HAMLET

How chances it they travel? their residence both in reputation and profit was better both ways.

ROSENCRANTZ

I think their inhibition comes by the means of the late innovation.

HAMLET

Do they hold the same estimation they did when I was in the city; are they so followed?

ROSENCRANTZ

No, indeed, are they not.

HAMLET

How comes it? do they grow rusty?

ROSENCRANTZ

Nay, their endeavour keeps in the wonted pace; but there is, sir, an aery of children, little eyases, that cry out on the top of question, and are most tyrannically clapped for't: these are now the fashion, and so berattle the common stages (so they call them) that many wearing rapiers are afraid of goose-quills, and dare scarce come thither.

HAMLET

What, are they children? who maintains 'em? how are they escoted? Will they pursue the quality no longer than they can sing? will they not say afterwards if they should grow themselves to common players (as it is like most will if their means are not better) their writers do them wrong, to make them exclaim against their own succession?

ROSENCRANTZ

Faith, there has been much to-do on both sides: and the nation holds it no sin to tarre them to controversy. There was, for a while, no money bid for argument, unless the Poet and the Player went to cuffs in the question.

HAMLET

Is't possible?

GUILDENSTERN

O, there has been much throwing about of brains.

HAMLET

Do the boys carry it away?

ROSENCRANTZ

Ay, that they do, my lord, Hercules and his load too.

(ACT II, SCENE 2)

This passage now reads:

HAMLET

... What players are they?

ROSENCRANTZ

Even those you used to take such delight in, the tragedians of the city.

HAMLET

How does it happen that they are touring? Do they hold the same esteem as they did when I was in the city? Are they as popular?

ROSENCRANTZ

No, indeed, they are not.

HAMLET

How come? Have they grown rusty?

ROSENCRANTZ

No, they are as good as ever; but there are now in the city companies of children, little boy-actors, who are most extravagantly applauded; these are now the fashion.

HAMLET

Is it possible? . . . And the boys win the day?

ROSENCRANTZ

Ay, that they do, my lord.

Here is another pasage—Hamlet asking the First Player to recite a dramatic speech, part of which Hamlet remembers:

HAMLET

"The rugged Pyrrhus, he whose sable arms,
Black as his purpose, did the night resemble
When he lay couchéd in the ominous horse,
Hath now this dread and black complexion smeared
With heraldry more dismal: head to foot
Now is he total gules, horridly tricked
With blood of fathers, mothers, daughters, sons,
Baked and impasted with the parching streets,
That lend a tyrannous and a damnéd light
To their lord's murder. Roasted in wrath and fire,
And thus o'er-sizéd with coagulate gore,
With eyes like carbunclés, the hellish Pyrrhus
Old grandsire Priam seeks" . . .
So proceed you.

POLONIUS

'Fore God, my lord, well spoken, with good accent and good discretion.

FIRST PLAYER

        "Anon he finds him
Striking too short at Greeks, his antique sword,
Rebellious to his arm, lies where it falls,

Repugnant to command; unequal matched,
Pyrrhus at Priam drives, in rage strikes wide,
But with the whiff and wind of his fell sword
Th' unnervéd father falls: then senseless Ilium,
Seeming to feel this blow, with flaming top
Stoops to his base; and with a hideous crash
Takes prisoner Pyrrhus' ear. For lo! his sword,
Which was declining on the milky head
Of reverend Priam, seemed i' th' air to stick,
So as a painted tyrant Pyrrhus stood,
And like a neutral to his will and matter,
Did nothing:
But as we often see, against some storm,
A silence in the heavens, the rack stand still,
The bold winds speechless, and the orb below
As hush as death, anon the dreadful thunder
Doth rend the region, so after Pyrrhus' pause,
A rouséd vengeance sets him new awork,
And never did the Cyclops' hammers fall
On Mars's armour, forged for proof eterne,
With less remorse than Pyrrhus' bleeding sword
Now falls on Priam.
Out, out, thou strumpet Fortune! All you gods,
In general synod take away her power,
Break all the spokes and fellies from her wheel,
And bowl the round nave down the hill of heaven
As low as to the fiends."

POLONIUS

This is too long.

(ACT II, SCENE 2)

I think for once Polonius is right. So now the scene reads:

HAMLET

"The rugged Pyrrhus—he whose mighty shield,
Black as his purpose, did the night resemble
When he lay hidden in the ominous horse—
With eyes like carbuncles old Priam seeks."
So, proceed.

POLONIUS

By God, my lord, well spoken; with good accent and
good discretion.

FIRST PLAYER

        "And then he finds him
Striking too short at Greeks; his antique sword,
Rebellious to his arm, lies where it falls,
Repugnant to command. Unequal matched,
Pyrrhus at Priam drives; in rage strikes wide;
But with the whiff and wind of his dread sword
The unnerved father falls. Pyrrhus stood still;
Did nothing.
But as we often see, before some storm,
A silence in the heavens, the clouds stand still,
The bold winds speechless, and the earth below
As hush as death, and then the dreadful thunder
Does rend the air; so after Pyrrhus' pause
His risen vengeance sets him anew to work;
And never did the Cyclops' hammers fall
On Mars's armour, forged for proof eternal,
With less remorse than Pyrrhus' bleeding sword
Now falls on Priam.
Out, out, thou strumpet Fortune!"

POLONIUS

This is too long.

I have also cut out some lines which Shakespeare wrote only because of the nature and requirements of the Elizabethan stage. As we know, the stage in the Globe theatre protruded into the courtyard, had no curtain, no sets, no side wings. This made it necessary for Shakespeare to include in the dialogue certain lines which today, with our kind of stage, are unnecessary.

For example, let us take the last speech in the play:

FORTINBRAS

Let four captains
Bear Hamlet, like a soldier, to the stage;
For he was likely, had he been put on,
To have proved most royal; and, for his passage,
The soldiers' music and the rites of war
Speak loudly for him.
Take up the bodies: such a sight as this
Becomes the field, but here shows much amiss.
Go, bid the soldiers shoot.

Lines 6 and 7 in the above

Take up the bodies: such a sight as this
Becomes the field, but here shows much amiss.

are an anticlimactic and rather pedestrian intrusion into the lofty tribute Fortinbras pays Hamlet. Shakespeare had to include them in order to clear the stage of all the dead bodies at the end of a performance. There was no final curtain to hide them from the spectators. Nor would it do, of course, to see those corpses lying there until the audience had left the theatre or, worse, have them come back to life again to take their bows.

Today, when we can use the curtain or dim out the lights, these lines are superfluous. Their elimination improves the final speech in the tragedy.

I have also made some cuts which have to do with so-called asides and the few cues in the original text which call for specific actions on the stage.

Hamlet has been more or less constantly produced in theatres ever since its successful opening at the Globe over three and a half centuries ago. As happens in other fields of human endeavor performed through a long span of time, this has gradually created a number of traditions. These have been fairly consistently maintained in performances of *Hamlet*. A number of these traditions I find wrong and unfitting. So I have changed some and eliminated others. Here again, I am convinced that these were not originated by Shakespeare, and were he to witness them, he would censure them.

First, the Asides.

ASIDES / We know that *asides* are an old theatrical convention, now rarely used, which denotes that words or passages so marked are the character's inner thoughts, expressed for the benefit of the audience, but not heard by other persons on the stage. When lines are marked *Aside to*— it means that they are heard only by the person addressed and not by anyone else present in the scene.

I think that some of the asides in *Hamlet* have been wrongly defined as such; they should be part of the straight dialogue. These asides must have gradually crept into the performance through the initiative of actors. This is quite probable—the predilection of some actors frequently to address their lines directly to the audience instead of the characters on the stage, for whom they are intended, is well known. Subsequently these arbitrarily created asides found their way into the published text and became crystallized into traditions.

An example—Hamlet is talking to Polonius about Ophelia:

HAMLET

Let her not walk in the sun. Conception is a blessing, but not as your daughter may conceive. Friend, look to it.

POLONIUS (*Aside*)

What say you by that? Still harping on my daughter; yet he knew me not at first; . . .

(ACT II, SCENE 2)

Now, Hamlet has made a most alarming insinuation. I feel that the first sentence of Polonius' speech would be spontaneously addressed to Hamlet, and only the rest delivered as an aside:

POLONIUS (*to* HAMLET)

What say you by that? (*Aside*) Still harping on my daughter; . . .

Another example. In the scene between Hamlet, Rosencrantz and Guildenstern, Hamlet conjures his former friends:

. . . be honest and direct with me, whether you were sent for, or not.

ROSENCRANTZ (*Aside to* GUILDENSTERN)

What do you say?

HAMLET (*Aside*)

Nay, then, I have an eye on you. If you love me, do not
hold off.

GUILDENSTERN

My lord, we were sent for.

(ACT II, SCENE 2)

Both of the above asides should be direct, natural dialogue. This makes the passage more dramatic and effective.

And one more example—from "the play-within-the-
play":

PLAYER QUEEN

In second husband let me be accurst!
None wed the second but who killed the first.

HAMLET (*Aside*)

Wormwood, wormwood!

(ACT III, SCENE 2)

Hamlet's exclamation here means little as an aside, but
if addressed directly to the King and Queen it becomes a
pointed and bold provocation. I am sure that Shakespeare meant
Hamlet to do just that.

(Above quotations are phrased as in the present revised
text, not the standard one.)

ACTING TRADITIONS / Now to touch on some acting traditions
in *Hamlet*. In a few spots of the original text a specific action is
indicated either by dialogue or by a curt direction. Some of
these I have modified, some I have eliminated. Those that have

been modified can be observed in this revised version through the different stage directions which have been supplied.

Here are a few examples of ones I have eliminated:

In Act I, Scene 5, Hamlet, after his fateful and soul-shattering encounter with the Ghost, speaks a soliloquy which ends with:

> My tables! Meet it is I set it down
> That one may smile, and smile, and be a villain;
> At least I'm sure it may be so in Denmark.
> So, uncle, there you are. Now to my word:
> It is "Adieu, adieu! Remember me."
> I have sworn't.

To us the words "My tables!" in this context are obscure, if not misleading. *Tables* meant "notebook." In Shakespeare's time it was the fashion for young gentlemen, especially of the nobility, to carry on their persons a handy little notebook. Whenever they heard, in a theatre or at a social gathering, a quip or a witticism they thought worth remembering, they would then and there inscribe it in their notebook.

So, Hamlet's exclamation "My tables!" meant "My notebook!" and, as the next line indicates, was followed by Hamlet taking his out and writing in it the thought stirred in him by the Ghost and the Ghost's final admonition. To an Elizabethan audience this action seemed natural and understandable. To us it would appear both unexpected and silly, especially so under the tragic and "occult" circumstances of this scene. Therefore I have revised the first line to read:

> Ay, meet it is for me to set it down . . .

Another example. After the murder of Polonius, the King sends Rosencrantz and Guildenstern, accompanied by

Guards, to seek and bring Hamlet to him. They find Hamlet and, after some dialogue, tell him that he must go with them to the King. This is followed by:

HAMLET

The body is with the King, but the King is not with the body. The King is a thing . . .

GUILDENSTERN

A thing, my lord?

HAMLET

Of nothing. Bring me to him. Hide fox, and all after.

(OLD ACT IV, SCENE 3)

The words "Hide fox, and all after" have reference to the fox hunt, and here, as a rule, Hamlet suddenly breaks into a run, presumably trying to escape, and is followed offstage by Rosencrantz, Guildenstern, and the Guards at full gallop, brandishing their swords in the air.

I find this utterly unfitting to the character of Hamlet, to his sense of dignity. The action is futile, foolish, and embarrassing. Yes, Hamlet does at times *act* the fool, when he assumes his "antique disposition," but he never *is* a fool.

I am sure that Hamlet's line "Hide fox, and all after," and the clumsy action that follows it, is not Shakespeare's writing, but, again, a subsequent interpolation by an actor, possibly by Richard Burbage, who was the first to perform the role.

This is not unusual; it happens in the theatre all the time, today as frequently as in the past. For instance, King Richard's famous

A horse! a horse! my kingdom for a horse!

(*Richard III*, ACT V)

is considered by Shakespearean scholars an interpolation by David Garrick, perhaps the most famous English Hamlet, as well as the most reckless rewriter of that play. That particular interpolation happens to be a happy one, and does not demean Shakespeare, but that is not very often the case.

Many actors today, as in times past, seem irresistibly tempted to contribute to the writing of the play. So, now and then, they improvise a line they think is effective, and which they fortuitously keep in the text unless checked by the author or director. This is one of the liberties one must constantly watch out for, and, when it occurs, nip it in the bud. Shakespeare, on his own testimony, seems to have bitterly suffered from it. In his admonition to the Players Hamlet says:

> ... And let your comedians speak no more than is set down for them. For there are some of them that will themselves laugh, to set on a number of half-witted spectators to laugh too, though in the meantime some necessary question of the play is to be considered. That's villainous, and shows a most pitiful ambition in the fool that uses it.
>
> (ACT III, SCENE 2)

The reason Shakespeare puts the emphasis on comedians is because, of all actors, they are the ones most notoriously addicted to taking liberties with the text and making up their own, usually unsuitable, ad libs. For too many comedians the ultimate achievement is to make the audience laugh, and the louder the better. To them the end justifies the means, no matter how injurious these means may be to the play. The more laughs they get, the happier they are, even though these may be what we in the theatre call "wrong laughs" or "bad laughs." As a director, I have to deal with this phenomenon all too frequently.

To come back to "Hide fox, and all after"—I have eliminated that line from the text, and with it, naturally, the action it implies.

Another instance is in the well-known scene in the churchyard, where Hamlet, following the example of Laertes, leaps into the open grave of Ophelia and there struggles with him. Here again I am convinced that Hamlet's action is not intended by Shakespeare, and was initiated by an actor. Shakespeare is quite consistent in indicating through his dialogue, whenever possible, the specific action called for at the time. Laertes' leap into the grave is certainly part of Shakespeare's design. He makes it clear in so many words:

Laertes

. . . hold off the earth awhile,
Till I have caught her once more in mine arms.

(*leaps in the grave*)
Now pile your dust upon the quick and dead, . . .

Laertes' leap is made explicit here, the words themselves confirming the stage direction.

Now listen to Hamlet's speech, which follows:

Hamlet

What is he whose grief
Bears such an emphasis? whose phrase of sorrow
Conjures the wand'ring stars, and makes them stand
Like wonder-wounded bearers? This is I,
Hamlet the Dane.   (*leaps in after Laertes*)
(OLD ACT V, SCENE I)

The two then indulge in a wrestling match inside Ophelia's grave, presumably trampling her body under their feet.

[3 1]

I cannot conceive of greater callousness or vulgarity. Furthermore, this action ceases to be drama and becomes tawdry burlesque. It is hard to believe that Shakespeare could have devised it. Laertes' action is valid, because it stems naturally from his character. With Hamlet, it is a shockingly jarring note. He is by temperament incapable of behaving in such execrable taste. And there is further concrete proof in the speech Shakespeare puts into Hamlet's mouth here (quoted above). It is deliberate and controlled. The first three lines are full of withering contempt for Laertes; and the last line is one of quiet, majestic dignity:

> This is I,
> Hamlet the Dane.

For the first time in the play Hamlet speaks of himself as the King of Denmark ("the Dane"), the office that was his due by right and inheritance and out of which he was cheated by his uncle. It is impossible to imagine that any person, let alone Hamlet, at the moment he assumes the lofty dignity of his royal title, would immediately proceed to behave like a brawling private in the ranks.

To ascribe this to Shakespeare is absurd and insulting. At the same time, all the natural earmarks of an actor's interpolation are present here. The majority of actors, some of the most gifted among them, are possessed of a race-horse instinct which is very difficult for them to control (that is why for the good of the play, as well as their own, the reins should be firmly held by the director). This instinct manifests itself in the actor's effort to outrun all other performers in every scene of the play. It is especially true of some stars, with the result that they end up giving a grandiose solo performance in a seemingly unpopulated vacuum of the stage, very much to the detriment of the whole play. Now, the role of Laertes is very effective and showy—he is written by Shakespeare as an athletic, impetuous youth, unbridled in his passions, reckless in his behavior, full of sound and fury, and prone to exhibitionism. So the actor playing Laertes usually has a field day and sinks his teeth into the part with abandon. Furthermore, he does so, ferociously, because throughout the performance he resents the fact that he is not playing Hamlet himself. For this reason, the Hamlet of the play usually keeps a wary eye on Laertes and makes special efforts not to be outdone by him in scenes which involve them both. Thus, it is easy to imagine how, when an early Laertes took his flamboyant leap into Ophelia's grave, as prescribed by Shakespeare, Hamlet, not to be outdone, followed suit, impelled by his own spontaneous though misdirected impulse. So, a wrong precedent was established; it later became traditional and was included in the original published text: [Hamlet] *leaps in after Laertes.*

I have eliminated this stage direction from the present version.

SPELLING, PRONUNCIATION / Modern spelling has been substituted for words spelled differently at the time of Shakespeare's writing; most of the words which had to be pronounced as bisyllables to sustain the rhythm of the verse have been rearranged, so that now they can be accented in the usual manner. For instance:

MARCELLUS

Some say that ever 'gainst that season comes
Wherein our Saviour's birth is celebrated,
The bird of dawning singéth all night long, . . .

(ACT I, SCENE I)

[3 3]

P. H. WELSHIMER MEMORIAL LIBRARY
MILLIGAN COLLEGE, TENN. 37682

Now it is:

> Some say that ever when that season comes
> Wherein our Saviour's birth is celebrated,
> The bird of dawning sings throughout the night . . .

And:

QUEEN

> Good Hamlet, cast thy nighted colour off,
> And let thine eye look like a friend on Denmark,
> Do not for ever with thy vailéd lids
> Seek for thy noble father in the dust,
> Thou know'st 'tis common, all that lives must die, . . .

(ACT I, SCENE 2)

This now reads:

> Good Hamlet, cast your nighted colour off,
> And let your eye look like a friend on Denmark.
> Do not for ever with your down-cast lids
> Seek for your noble father in the dust.
> You know it's common, all that lives must die, . . .

Another phrase:

CAPTAIN

> Truly to speak, and with no additión,
> We go to gain a little patch of ground . . .

(ACT IV, SCENE 4)

[34]

It now is:

> Truly to speak, with no exaggeration,
> We go to gain a little patch of ground . . .
>
> (NOW ACT III, SCENE 8)

PUNCTUATION / In modifying the punctuation I have followed my judgment and my experience with the spoken word in the theatre. My object was to help bring out the proper meaning of the lines, and make their reading and speaking easier, more intelligible, and more effective.

REARRANGING *HAMLET* INTO FOUR ACTS

The original publication of *Hamlet* as we know it, Quarto-2 of 1604, contained no divisions whatsoever into acts and scenes; the play proceeded in uninterrupted continuity. Folio-1 indicated only "Act I. Scene 1," "Scene 2," "Scene 3," "Act II," "Scene 2"—that was all. The numbering of acts and scenes in the play was the work of a later editor, Nicholas Rowe, who divided *Hamlet* into five acts, and grouped the scenes accordingly (1709). This arrangement is arbitrary and does not fit the progress of action. Yet, for some strange reason, it has persisted and become traditional. All subsequent published versions have perpetuated it.

If we must divide *Hamlet* into acts, we might as well do it as suitably as possible, bearing in mind the psychology of audiences and the logic of theatrical intermissions in a play.

With dramas which follow the three classical unities, the manner in which they are divided into acts is not so important as it is with the more modern forms of playwriting, which cover a variety of locations and extensive time.

[3 5]

The period of time covered by the story in *Hamlet* is a little over two and one-half months. That part of it which is actually shown to us through dialogue and action while the curtain is up takes place during four and one-half days. The balance of the time we do not witness on the stage—it is consumed by the intervals between the scenes and acts; it flows behind the closed curtain.

The standard arrangement of Act I and Act II is valid, but the traditional divisions of Acts III, IV, and V, and the grouping of scenes within them, are not satisfactory.

Let us observe the time continuity of the play's action in the last three acts—we can deduce it from the inner evidence of the drama, following the clues given by the dialogue.

Act III, Scene 1 begins the day after the end of Act II. Scene 2 takes place the evening of the same day. Scene 3 and Scene 4, which conclude Act III, and the first four scenes of Act IV follow each other in direct succession (there is just a few hours' interval between Scene 3 and Scene 4 of Act IV). Thus the intermission between Act III and Act IV breaks and arrests the fluid time-continuum of action. This kind of interruption is bad in the theatre. It is necessary, whenever possible, to see to it that the intervals between acts imply and coincide with passage of time, to avoid the impression that while you are smoking your cigarette during the intermission the action of the play is held at a standstill, awaiting your return to the auditorium. This is exactly what the standard break between Acts III and IV does. Act III ends with the scene between Hamlet and his mother in the Queen's bedroom, and Act IV begins with action which immediately follows that scene: the Queen reporting to the King on her session with Hamlet. Thus the usual intermission between Act III and Act IV interrupts the progression of the play and holds it in abeyance, as though all the characters onstage had been suddenly frozen into a tableau, waiting for the rise of the next act's curtain to come to life again.

The intermission between Acts IV and V is equally unsuitable. Within Act IV there is an implied passage of about ten days between Scene 4 and Scene 5. Yet these scenes follow each other on the stage directly without any actual time-lapse or curtain.

I think that reorganizing the last three acts into two makes it psychologically easier and more comfortable for the audience to follow the progress of the story, and makes for better showmanship.

That is why I have regrouped *Hamlet* into four acts.

Act III, which previously consisted of four scenes, now also includes the first four scenes of the old Act IV, so that the continuous stage action of these scenes flows without interruption.

Now the intermission between Act III and Act IV, the last one, covers a passage of about ten days. Act IV starts with what used to be Scene 5 of the old Act IV, and the action continues uninterrupted to the end of the play.

I felt that it would be of help to the reader and the spectator to be aware of the time sequence and intervals in *Hamlet*. I have therefore indicated at the beginning of each scene and each act the time lapses between them and the preceding ones.

THE AGES OF CHARACTERS IN THE PLAY

A MODERN playwright, in supplying us with the list of characters which usually precedes the text of the play, almost invariably specifies, for the benefit of the director and the actors, the age of each character. This information is vital to those who are to perform in the play. Its lack may badly affect both the casting and the interpretation of those characters, as it may confuse and mislead the reader. If this question were left to the discretion of the director, the actor, or the reader, it could easily result in distortions, not only of the characters involved but also of the basic meaning and intent of the play itself, as it was conceived by the dramatist. If a modern playwright has failed to indicate the ages of his characters, it is not quite so serious an omission as it would be with a play written a long time ago; we can ask him about it. If he is dead, we can make our own guess, and it would not be too far off, because we all have a common, present-day idea of what constitutes "young," "middle-aged," or "old." But, when we deal with a period play, we must remember that these terms have changed their meaning and no longer denote what they did in their time. For one thing, the average span of human life has steadily increased. Ophelia, Juliet, and Desdemona, for instance, were about fourteen years old. In Shakespeare's time they were considered young women and fit to be heroines in lofty tragedies—today we would call them children. Today a man of thirty is a young man; in Shakespeare's time he would have been middle-aged. Shakespeare, at the age of forty, considered himself an old man (Sonnets). To us his death at fifty-two seems shockingly premature, yet in the eyes of his contemporaries, so many of whom died much younger, he had a ripe, long life.

All this must be borne in mind when reading *Hamlet* and when casting it for the stage.

Shakespeare did not give us a specific list of characters indicating the age of each, but he certainly gave us an abundance of inner evidence in the play itself, which makes it easy enough for us to figure it out for ourselves.

The most important, quite naturally, is Hamlet—his age would tell us pretty accurately how old all the other important characters are.

HAMLET'S AGE / Hamlet is supposed to be thirty years old—
for this we have precise information supplied by Shakespeare
himself, in two places, both in the later sections of the play:
the first in "the play-within-the-play," in Act III, Scene 2; the
second in the graveyard, in the old Act V, Scene 1.

We will take up the latter first, because it is definitive.
Hamlet is talking to the First Gravedigger:

HAMLET

. . . How long hast thou been a grave-maker?

FIRST GRAVEDIGGER

Of all the days i' the year, I came to't that day that our
last king Hamlet overcame Fortinbras.

HAMLET

How long is that since?

FIRST GRAVEDIGGER

Cannot you tell that? Every fool can tell that. It was the
very day that young Hamlet was born. . . .

FIRST GRAVEDIGGER

. . . I have been sexton here, man and boy, thirty years.

This clearly specifies Hamlet's age as thirty.

The second, contributory evidence occurs in the first
speech of the Player King in "the play-within-the-play" (Act
III, Scene 2):

PLAYER KING

Full *thirty* times hath Phoebus' cart gone round
Neptune's salt wash and Tellus' orbéd ground,

And *thirty* dozen moons with borrowed sheen
About the world have times twelve *thirties* been,
Since love our hearts, and Hymen did our hands,
Unite commutual in most sacred bands.

(Italics are mine.)

Thirty, repeated here three times, obviously refers to Hamlet's age. In my opinion, the above speech is part of the mysterious "dozen or sixteen lines" which Hamlet inserted into "the play-within-the-play." The deliberate reiteration of "thirty" here is for the purpose of letting King Claudius and Queen Gertrude know at the very outset that the Player King and Player Queen are meant to represent Hamlet's father and mother.

Thus, on Shakespeare's own word, Hamlet is thirty years old.

Most readers, actors, and critics accept this, and let it go at that. However, many others have been for a long time puzzled, and are still confounded by Hamlet's age. They feel that there are many other indications in the play which convey the strong impression that Hamlet is a much younger man, possibly a youth of nineteen. This creates a puzzle. A number of critics, among them some of the most reputable, finding themselves unable to resolve it, take the easiest way out. Following the line of least resistance, they dismiss the whole matter of Hamlet's age as immaterial and irrelevant. They overlook, or do not sufficiently appreciate, the fact that *Hamlet* is a *play*, written for the purpose of being *performed* on the stage. They fail to realize that Hamlet himself is not merely a theoretical conception, an abstract figure in a dream, but a living, smoldering character in a living, smoldering drama. No actor can perform Hamlet and no reader can read him intelligently without knowing how old he is.

The critics who feel that Hamlet's age is of concern are confused by the riddle it presents in the play. One must admit that in this case, and it is an exception, Shakespeare himself is responsible. On one hand, as we mentioned, he makes a deliberate point of specifying that Hamlet is thirty (which, incidentally, he rarely does with his characters); on the other hand, his play is full of inner evidence which qualifies Hamlet as a youth of nineteen or twenty. Thus we have a glaring contradiction, generated by the author himself. It creates in the minds of critics a kind of double exposure. Because of this seemingly insoluble dichotomy of Hamlet's image, some of the critics have been moved to make rather unwise conjectures and explanations. One, based on their hobby horse—Shakespeare's "thoughtlessness" and "inconsistency"—ascribes the whole thing to simple negligence, an oversight on the author's part. Another, just as invalid, maintains that when Shakespeare began writing the play he had conceived Hamlet as a youth, and treated him as such in the early scenes, but as the play progressed, he realized that he was endowing Hamlet with an intellect and depth of thought beyond the capacity of so young a person. Therefore, presumably, in the latter portions of the play he transformed Hamlet into a man thirty years old. This kind of erratic, clumsy conception wouldn't be worthy of a third-rate playwright, let alone Shakespeare. It would also mean that the action of the play consumes at least ten years, which is patently ridiculous.

We face a dilemma presented by the author himself. We must resolve it by deciding which of his own two conflicting bodies of evidence is more important and valid: the numerous references and inner clues indicating that Hamlet is a youth of about twenty, or the isolated statement, oddly overemphasized and appearing toward the end of the play, that he is a man of thirty.

The confusion about Hamlet's age, on one side, and the assumption that he is thirty years old, on the other, are responsible for many inconsistencies, contradictions, and so-called mysteries which the critics find in the play, and which are accepted now by most people as facts.

A thirty-year-old Hamlet puts the whole tragedy out of focus.

I submit that, beyond a shadow of reasonable doubt, Hamlet is about twenty years old—that is how Shakespeare conceived him, wrote him, and meant him to be throughout the play.

I have therefore revised his age accordingly, by replacing every "thirty" in both segments quoted above with "twenty."

In view of the fact that this correction appears to be a contradiction of Shakespeare's own words, allow me to present the overwhelming evidence which justifies it—Shakespeare's evidence, not mine.

To start with, let us note the manner in which the other characters in the play refer to Hamlet.

The very first mention of him is by Horatio, at the end of the first scene:

Let us impart what we have seen tonight
Unto young Hamlet.

Now, if Hamlet's father, whose name was also Hamlet, were still living, we could consider that Horatio is using "young" in the sense of "junior," to distinguish the son from the father. But King Hamlet is dead. Therefore, "young" here distinctly refers to Hamlet's age. And let us firmly bear in mind what "young" meant in Shakespeare's time.

Laertes talking to Ophelia:

For Hamlet, and the trifling of his favour,
Hold it a fashion, and a toy in blood;
A violet in the youth of primy nature, . . .

(ACT I, SCENE 3)

These lines beautifully describe the passing fancy of a youth,
but apply them to a man of thirty, and they become ludicrous.
In the same scene, Polonius to Ophelia:

For Lord Hamlet,
Believe so much in him, that he is young, . . .

The Ghost to Hamlet:

. . . but know, thou noble youth, . . .

(ACT I, SCENE 5)

Ophelia, referring to Hamlet:

That unmatched form and feature of blown youth.

(ACT III, SCENE I)

Polonius to the Queen:

Tell him his pranks have been too broad to bear with, . . .

(ACT III, SCENE 4)

The King:

This mad young man . . .

(ACT IV, SCENE I)

[43]

And Hamlet's own words:

Yea, from the table of my memory
I'll wipe away all trivial fond records,
All saws of books, all forms, all pressures past
That youth and observation copied there, . . .

(ACT I, SCENE 5)

In these quotations Hamlet's youth is literally spelled out. But there is other voluminous and weightier inner testimony in the play which does not mention Hamlet's "youth" in so many words, but certainly indicates and expresses it fully and unmistakably.

In the first introduction of Hamlet (Act I, Scene 2) King Claudius, in front of the whole court assembled in formal session, reprimands, or rather excoriates, Hamlet for his continued mourning of his father. He does this in terms that would be unthinkable if Hamlet were not a very young man. The King's speech starts with:

'Tis sweet and commendable in your nature, Hamlet,
To give these mourning duties to your father; . . .

Later:

'Tis unmanly grief;
It shows a will most incorrect to heaven,
A heart unfortified, a mind impatient,
An understanding simple and unschooled; . . .

And:

Fie! 'tis a fault to heaven,
A fault against the dead, a fault to nature,
To reason most absurd, . . .

[44]

And then:

> For your intent
> In going back to school in Wittenberg,
> It is most retrograde to our desire; . . .

Just imagine Hamlet being thirty years old, and see how unfitting and implausible those lines become.

Also, we discover here that Hamlet wants to return to his school in Wittenberg. As we later learn, he came home from there because of his father's death, presumably interrupting his studies. This would be hard to accept even if it concerned some slow-witted man of thirty, let alone a brilliant intellect like Hamlet.

In Act I, Scene 5, Hamlet to the Ghost:

> Haste me to know't, that I, with wings as swift
> As meditation or the thoughts of love,
> May sweep to my revenge.

This sounds beautifully apt and right when uttered by a romantic youth, but would be quite uncomfortable put into the mouth of a thirty-year-old man, especially in the given circumstances.

In the same scene, Hamlet's famous passage:

> O villain, villain, smiling, damnéd villain!
> My tables! Meet it is I set it down
> That one may smile, and smile, and be a villain;
> At least I'm sure it may be so in Denmark.

It is difficult to imagine this discovery being made by a man of thirty, even if he had spent his life in an ivory tower and suffered from arrested development to boot. But how true, how sadly reminiscent it is to all of us, when expressed by a sensitive youth, who suddenly, and for the first time, gets his teeth knocked out, figuratively speaking, by life, and who is shocked to discover that callous hypocrisy exists in this world. This is so foreign to Hamlet's nature that he makes it a point not to forget it in the future. And how touchingly young and endearing is his last remark: "At least I'm sure it may be so in Denmark." So great is his innate nobility and his optimism (the latter doomed to be smashed by the events) that he still believes such villainy may only exist in Denmark, and not in the rest of the world.

The signs of Hamlet's youth are just as consistently present in the final sections of the play.

For instance, in the churchyard (Act V, Scene 1) Hamlet, astounded that a Gravedigger can blithely sing a love-ballad while digging a grave, asks Horatio:

Has this fellow no feeling of his business, that he sings at grave-making?

Horatio explains:

Custom hath made it in him a property of easiness.
[Meaning: Custom has made him easy in it.]

Here Hamlet, a genius, with the keenest insight into the workings of the human mind, has to be enlightened by Horatio, who is far from being his intellectual peer. This again indicates Hamlet's youth and his limited experience with the ordinary, practical affairs of the world. Horatio, because of his humbler station in life and his more common background, is much more familiar with them. It is my view that Horatio is a few years older than Hamlet; I feel it throughout the play. His attitude seems one of deep affection and loyalty toward a Prince who is somewhat younger than he.

There is, in addition, throughout the play a continuous line of important inner evidence which attests to Hamlet's youth. It is observed in his emotional experiences, in some of his thinking, and in his behavior. Let me mention some of it.

We find Hamlet meditating on the subject of suicide, and even wishing for death. This is natural and not at all unexpected in a sensitive, idealistic youth whose whole world has suddenly collapsed into ruin, who has suffered a bitter disillusionment in everyone he had thought pure, good, and noble. It is just as if life had been wearing a glowingly beautiful mask, which now is torn away to expose a hideous skull. The shock of this to any young man of twenty would be cataclysmic. I think that most thoughtful youths in every generation, including ours, have had this kind of crucial experience. Many of us remember that moment in our own youth when a cruel blow shattered our best illusions, things most precious to us, and made us feel for a while that this world was not worth living in. Does one not then give a thought to suicide? I know I did when I was nineteen. Of course, most of us give it a thought and then get over it. This is Hamlet's case, and as a very young man, he has not only our understanding but our empathy. It would be quite different if Hamlet were thirty. Then we might rightly think of him as a man suffering from extreme neurotic complexes.

There is another circumstance which bears on Hamlet's age. He is the rightful heir to the throne of Denmark and has been done out of it by his uncle Claudius. Young Hamlet certainly resents this loss and injury, but his reaction to it is rather moderate. Now, were Hamlet thirty years old, Claudius may not have dared to usurp the crown. Or if he had, that older Hamlet would not have stood for it, and would have been better able to put up a public fight for his royal inheritance.

Hamlet's youth also clarifies and explains several phases in his behavior which seem to confuse, puzzle, and—in some cases—appall almost all critics. I am referring to the hue and cry raised on the subject of Hamlet's behavior toward his mother, his supposedly excessive reaction to the adultery and incest she has committed, and his allegedly gross and cruel treatment of Ophelia. I submit that Hamlet's strong reactions in both cases are justified and natural in a deeply sensitive youth. If Hamlet were thirty, then the critics would be right. Many of his attitudes would then be too immature and disproportionate to his age.

Actually, once it is established that Hamlet is a youth of twenty, many inconsistencies, contradictions, and "mysteries" against which critics seem constantly to be bumping their heads dissolve into thin air. With a young Hamlet the whole tragedy acquires a new, spontaneous life; it flows freely, naturally, and inevitably; and it gains immeasurably in truth and impact. *Hamlet* is a tragedy of youth. Yet in the last hundred years, it has been transformed by critics and performers into a play about middle-aged people.

Most critics not only accept Hamlet as a man of thirty, but maintain that he could not possibly be any younger. Their one "incontrovertible" argument is that no youth of twenty could possess so high an intellect, such keen perception, richness of thought, power of language—etc., etc.

The answer is simple: Hamlet is not just a young man of twenty, he is a *genius* of twenty. The reasoning of these critics on this point is as foolish as that of the lunatic fringe of Shakespearean dabblers who waste time, ink, and paper trying desperately, for a reason impossible for a sane man to follow, to prove that Shakespeare did not write his plays, that someone higher born and better educated did it for him. I would invite them to mention a single person in all of man's history who has *achieved* genius through inheriting a title or through education. A genius is born, not manufactured.

A genius differs from his fellow men not so much in his emotional make-up as in his intellectual and artistic powers. Even to him, emotional maturity comes gradually with age and experience. Hamlet's intellect, his intuition, and his powers of observation and creative expression are those of a genius. His emotions are basically those of a sensitive young man of twenty. In this respect he has not matured yet. And that is part of his tragedy.

Thus, to sum up, I find that everything in *Hamlet* portrays its hero as a youth. And nothing in it contradicts this; that is, nothing except a few words written by Shakespeare himself. I still have to face that.

The first publication of *Hamlet* was in 1603, and is known as Quarto-1. Its title reads:

THE
Tragicall Historie of
HAMLET
Prince of Denmarke
By William Shake-speare.
As it hath beene diuerse times acted by his Highnesse ser-
uants in the Cittie of London : as also in the two Vniuer-
sities of Cambridge and Oxford, and elsewhere.

It is not *Hamlet* as we know it today (the *Hamlet* of Quarto-2 and Folio-1), but a much shorter, rather elementary and garbled version. It was very badly printed too. Some critics feel that this is a pirated and barbarously distorted transcript of the standard *Hamlet;* that it was probably taken down during performances, or written later from memory, by someone who wanted to cash in on the popular success of that production at the Globe, by publishing it ahead of the author or the theatre's management. Other critics, while agreeing with most of this, are convinced that it is a badly pirated record, not of the *Hamlet* we know, but of the earlier, shorter, and much less masterful version which Shakespeare himself first wrote.

I definitely agree with the latter opinion—for many reasons which would be space-consuming and not relevant to the present discussion. This early draft of *Hamlet* was, to the best of our knowledge, written by Shakespeare about four years before he rewrote it, around 1601. The Quarto-2 was published in 1604 with the title:

THE
Tragicall Historie of
HAMLET
Prince of Denmarke.
By William Shakespeare.
Newly imprinted and enlarged to almost as much againe as it was, according to the true and perfect Coppie.

Shakespeare's first, short *Hamlet* played for several seasons at the Globe, and evidently enjoyed great success and popularity. This may have been part of Shakespeare's reason for wanting to amplify and improve it, which he did so magnificently.

Both in the first version and in the second, the role of Hamlet was played by Richard Burbage, a star in Shakespeare's company.

Richard Burbage was born about 1567—he was about three years younger than Shakespeare. He started acting "as soon

as he learned to speak." At twenty-one he was already a promi-
nent actor, and later became the most famous tragedian in England. He died on March 13, 1619 (three years after Shakespeare—
both men died at fifty-two).

Hamlet in Shakespeare's early version of the play
(Quarto-1) is about nineteen years old. Although his exact age
is not mentioned anywhere in the text, there is not the slightest
doubt about it. Everything in the play depicts and points to
a youth.

When Burbage first played this Hamlet, he was about
thirty. Being a great actor he undoubtedly succeeded in making
himself much younger on the stage.

While Shakespeare was rewriting this first version into
the masterpiece we know as *Hamlet*, he certainly was again
counting on his leading tragedian to play it. The hero of this
fuller and incomparably richer play was still a youth of nineteen
or twenty, but now he was endowed with genius. Only a great
actor could play him adequately.

As soon as Shakespeare finished writing with his goose-
quill the last word in his manuscript, he handed it to Burbage.

Before I relate what I think must have happened after
that, I wish to bring up a point here which is pertinent to clearer
understanding of what followed. It has to do with the casting
of a play. Professionals know it well, but laymen, to whom we
in the theatre are often prone to refer as "civilians," may not be
familiar with it.

In proper casting, the age of an actor in relation to the
character he is to play is as important as his acting ability and
personality; and by "age" I mean either his actual age or one
he can convincingly assume on the stage. We must bear in
mind that the text of a play is a piece of dramatic literature, and
does not become "theatre" until performed on the stage. Even
so, the written part, although it creates an image in the mind of

the reader, does not factually come to life until played by a particular actor. When this happens, it ceases to be solely what the dramatist has written, and inevitably becomes a combination of the writing with the personality and talent of the actor. An ideal performance is that which achieves a complete fusion of the two: the role and the performer. But ideal casting is very rare. If a dramatic manuscript had to wait for an ideal cast, it would probably never get produced. Most of the time one has to make reasonable compromises; in fact, it is only through these that one can achieve the best possible performance. The quickest way to accomplish the opposite is by expecting the actor rigidly to conform with every detailed requirement of the part. To make an oversimplified comparison: there is no perfect suit or dress in the abstract; it can only be perfect when it properly fits the man or woman who wears it. The same is true of casting and directing a performance—once you have selected the actor who best fits the character and have helped him to remold himself into the author's image to the limit of his capability, then you should go back to the script and modify the writing of the role as much as necessary to make it, in turn, fit the actor. This is a fruitful two-way compromise. The age of a character in a play is one of the elements that sometimes need such modification.

Directors have to deal with this contingency quite frequently, both on the stage and on the screen. Let me cite a few instances from my own professional experience.

In the play by Romain Rolland, *The Game of Love and Death*, we cast a very fine actor, Arthur Byron, to play the lead opposite Alice Brady. He was chronologically too old for the part, but we hoped this could be cured through performance. It did not happen. So, most reluctantly, we had to replace him with Frank Conroy, also one of our best actors.

In the film *Queen Christina* we wanted to cast John Barrymore in the lead opposite Greta Garbo, and he was most anxious to play it. But on further consideration we regretfully realized that he was a bit too old for it. Then we thought of a young English actor by the name of Laurence Olivier. I made a special test of him with Greta Garbo, using a scene from the script. He was too young. So he did not get the part—which did not stop him from growing into Sir Laurence Olivier. Ultimately, John Gilbert played the role.

In the motion picture *Golden Boy* we wanted to cast the leading role, that of a youthful violinist who becomes a prize-fighter, with some well-known star. Among these, only one was properly qualified—John Garfield; the others were too old. But Garfield was tied up at another studio. So finally, and with some fear and trepidation, I must confess, I selected a totally unknown and inexperienced youth whose name was William Holden.

I might mention here that the majority of actors and actresses do not consider themselves too old for almost any part, within reason. Optimism in regard to age and the feeling of being eternally young is a happy part of their make-up. But the opposite is also true. Many other fine and sensitive players refuse to play characters they consider much too young for themselves, for fear of appearing ridiculous. I remember when we were anxious to have Fred Astaire play the lead opposite Cyd Charisse in the musical film *Silk Stockings*. Mr. Astaire, an artist of great integrity and a perfectionist, liked the script very much, but did not wish to do it because he considered himself too old to play the part of the "lover." I succeeded in making him change his mind by pointing out that the character in the film need not be treated as a very young man, and further that Astaire himself, regardless of his chronological age, is younger and more attractive on the screen than most of today's so-called youthful stars.

But to return from the humble to the sublime: to Shakespeare, the author-director, and Burbage, his star-actor.

When Shakespeare handed his new *Hamlet* to Richard Burbage in 1601, Burbage was at least thirty-four—to the Elizabethans, a middle-aged man. Having read the script, Richard, enormously stirred, rushed back to his good friend and mentor, threw his hat on the floor in a gesture of admiration, embraced the master, and proclaimed that this was the greatest play Will had ever written, and Hamlet, the noblest and richest part ever to challenge an actor. "But . . ." said Richard—oh yes, he had a big *But*. He could not play it. This for a very obvious reason— he was much too old for it. Even while he performed Shakespeare's first *Hamlet*, some of his friends had made fun of him for trying to play at his ripe age a youth of nineteen—it would be even worse now that Richard was older. He would indeed be leading with his chin and inviting ridicule.

Now, to Shakespeare, no Richard meant no production of *Hamlet*. Nobody else in the company could possibly touch this role. (This is the kind of situation we frequently face today with certain plays and films—no star, no production.) Nothing Shakespeare said dissuaded Burbage. Oh yes, he was enraptured with the part, but could play it only if Hamlet were an older man.

Shakespeare knew that great actors are highly sensitive, their natural vanity easily hurt even by a casual slighting remark. Shakespeare also knew that under no condition would he agree to rewrite Hamlet as an older person. This would distort his whole design and artistic purpose. Yet he simply had to have Burbage; without him there would be no *Hamlet*. Also, he had more faith than did the actor himself that Burbage's talent could accomplish a youthful Hamlet on the stage. To resolve the impasse, Shakespeare said, all right, he would make Hamlet older; in fact, he would make him all of thirty—he would insert into the text several precise lines to that effect—and surely Richard, at thirty-four, could play thirty. Burbage pricked up his ears. However, said he, what about the whole tenor of the play? Everything in it portrays Hamlet as a youth. Shakespeare retorted that Richard was now being too finicky, unnecessarily concerned, and was underrating himself. Moreover, who could argue about Hamlet's age if the author himself indicated in the script that Hamlet is thirty years old?

Burbage could resist no longer. In his hands he held the weightiest and the greatest part ever written for an actor—he had to play it. So he agreed.

Thus it was that Shakespeare, acting under friendly duress, specified Hamlet's age as thirty—to save the star actor's face. But even at that, not to do violence to his work, nor to mislead the audience into a wrong conception of the play's hero, he inserted this specification into the very last act, where it came too late to do much harm.

The above is conjecture, of course. I don't imagine I could prove it in a court of law. However, allow me to say that the creative impulse is generated in the subconscious; that the truest and deepest values in great writing spring from the writer's intuition, his subconscious sources, and then are molded, with painstaking efforts, by his reason, his taste, and his powers of expression. I think that the reader, too, must allow his subconscious to function in order to understand rightly and fully the writer's work. That which stems from the writer's intuition can only be grasped by the reader's intuition. The reasoning process alone is not sufficient. And when a reader's intuitive perception stands the critical test of his reason, should it not then be as valid as fact? After all, don't we know from experience that spiritual truths cannot be perceived by purely cerebral calculations? Nor can they be proven.

AGES OF OTHER PRINCIPALS / I thought it helpful and necessary to specify, in the list which precedes the text of the play, the probable ages of all other important characters. You will note that they all are much younger than usually portrayed on the stage.

INSERTING STAGE DIRECTIONS

THE ORIGINAL texts of *Hamlet* (Quarto-2 and Folio-1) contained virtually no stage directions at all, not even the entrances and exits of the characters. To be specific, there were two or three entrances indicated, a few notations referring to music, and about seven brief directions relating to action. Even these were not by Shakespeare, but were undoubtedly inserted by the prompter and retained by the editors.

The fact that Shakespeare didn't bother to write any stage directions is neither odd nor unusual; in fact, it is quite natural, especially in his case. He was part-owner and manager of the theatre for which he wrote his plays; he wrote these for a permanent company of actors; he himself was an actor; and, even more important, he was also his own director. He conceived the staging of his play as he wrote it, he knew every bit of action he wanted in it, and then he, himself, directed the actors. For him to have bothered writing stage directions into his manuscript would have been a sheer waste of time. This, I believe, still holds true with most directors; at least I know it is true in my case. I personally never write stage directions into my working script —it is much easier, and saves me a lot of time, to keep them all in my head. As I direct the play in rehearsals, the stage manager writes them into the script. Subsequently, when that play is published, these stage directions become a necessary and important part of the text. They help the reader to visualize the play in action and to understand properly its meanings and its characters. Professionally, it is of great value to subsequent productions and revivals of the play. It makes their staging and interpretation much easier, naturally, and frequently keeps them from going astray.

The absence of stage directions in the publications of *Hamlet* is a great handicap, especially since *Hamlet* is more complex and difficult than any other drama. Why then should it not be published like any other modern play—with adequate and, possibly, revealing stage directions included in the text? This, again, would make it that much easier to follow, to understand, and to enjoy.

For this purpose I have written stage directions in this revised *Hamlet*. I have kept them as brief and sparse as possible, not to clutter the text and not to impede the flow of Shakespeare's word-music. I have put in just the minimum necessary to clarify the action and, in certain instances, to bring out the thoughts and emotions underlying the spoken lines.

I also hope that they may help dispel the obscurities, contradictions, and riddles which the critics keep ascribing to *Hamlet*, unjustly and with a persistence worthy of a better cause.

In conclusion, let me note that in revising the text of *Hamlet* I did not abide by rigid rules but followed my own taste and judgment; and, after all, this is the only possible criterion anyone can have when approaching a work of art.

I have assiduously avoided all personal notions and ideas that might be at variance with Shakespeare's concept, and tried to observe, discover, and sometimes divine, his own true meanings and intents. When a Raphael Madonna or Michelangelo's Sistine frescoes become grimy with the dust and erosions of centuries, they are carefully and lovingly restored to show anew their true designs and glowing colors. Similarly, my purpose was to free *Hamlet* from the accumulated barnacles of verbal archaisms, so that every reader can rediscover some of the hidden glories of Shakespeare and enjoy more abundantly "the proud full sail of his great verse."

R. M.

HAMLET

A New Version

Characters in the Play

CLAUDIUS, *King of Denmark, aged 45*

HAMLET, *Prince of Denmark, son of the late and nephew of the present King, aged 20*

POLONIUS, *Lord Chamberlain, aged 70*

HORATIO, *friend of Hamlet, aged 25*

LAERTES, *son of Polonius, aged 22*

VOLTEMAND, *aged 60*
CORNELIUS, *aged 55* } *Ambassadors to Norway*

ROSENCRANTZ, *aged 22*
GUILDENSTERN, *aged 23* } *Former fellow students of Hamlet*

OSRIC, *young Courtier, aged 17*

A GENTLEMAN

A PRIEST

MARCELLUS, *aged 21*
BERNARDO, *aged 22* } *Gentlemen of the Guard*
FRANCISCO, *aged 23*

REYNALDO, *servant of Polonius*

PLAYERS

FIRST GRAVEDIGGER

SECOND GRAVEDIGGER

FORTINBRAS, *Prince of Norway, aged 22*

A NORWEGIAN CAPTAIN

ENGLISH AMBASSADORS

GERTRUDE, *Queen of Denmark, mother of Hamlet, aged 38*

OPHELIA, *daughter of Polonius, aged 16*

Lords, Ladies, Officers, Soldiers, Sailors, Messengers, Attendants

The GHOST *of Hamlet's father, aged 55*

SCENE: *Elsinore, Denmark*

ACT I

A C T I

S C E N E 1

THE CASTLE AT ELSINORE. *A platform on the battlements.*
Cold night. Wisps of cloud and fog drift now and then
across the starry sky.

There is a hush, an inexplicable tension in the air. FRANCISCO,
the lone sentry, stands on duty—quite rigid. He is filled with
a vague sense of danger lurking in the dark around him.
For this he knows no reason. Bell O.S. starts beating mid-
night. BERNARDO, *the relieving sentry, enters—rather cau-*
tiously. He, too, is tense, but with good cause. As soon as
he catches sight of FRANCISCO, *who stands with his back to*
him, he stops dead in his tracks. His fear makes him break
the military rule:

BERNARDO

Who's there?
  (FRANCISCO *whirls around, lowering his halberd, ready*
  for an attack—it is his function, as sentry on guard,
  to challenge the comer:)

[6 5]

FRANCISCO
Nay, answer *me*! . . . Stand! and declare yourself.

BERNARDO
(*Relieved to hear a familiar voice*)

Long live the king!

FRANCISCO
Bernardo?

BERNARDO
Ay.

FRANCISCO
(*Equally relieved*)

You come most punctually upon your hour!

BERNARDO
(*Anxious to see* FRANCISCO *leave*)

It's now struck twelve; go on to bed, Francisco.

FRANCISCO
(*Puzzled by his own uneasiness*)

For this relief much thanks; it's bitter cold
And I am sick at heart.

BERNARDO
(*Alarmed, but tries not to show it*)

Have you had quiet guard?

FRANCISCO
                    Not a mouse stirring.

BERNARDO

Well, good night. (*Dreading to be left alone too long:*)
If you do meet Horatio and Marcellus,
The partners of my watch, bid them make haste.

FRANCISCO

I think I hear them. Stand! . . . Who's there?
(*Enter* HORATIO *and* MARCELLUS)

HORATIO

Friends to this ground.

MARCELLUS

And liegemen to the king.

FRANCISCO

Good night to you.

MARCELLUS

O, farewell, honest soldier.
(*Exit* FRANCISCO)

Holla! Bernardo!

BERNARDO

What, is Horatio there?

HORATIO

A piece of him.

BERNARDO

Welcome, Horatio; welcome, good Marcellus.

[6 7]

HORATIO

What, has this thing appeared again to-night?

BERNARDO

I have seen nothing.

MARCELLUS

Horatio says it's just our fantasy,
And will not let belief take hold of him
Touching this dreaded sight, twice seen by us.
Therefore I have entreated him along
With us to watch the minutes of this night,
That if again this apparition comes,
He may confirm our eyes, and speak to it.

HORATIO

Tush, tush, it won't appear.

MARCELLUS

         Sit down awhile;
And let us once again assail your ears,
That are so fortified against our story,
With what we've two nights seen.

HORATIO

         Well, sit we down,
And let us hear Bernardo speak of this.

BERNARDO

Last night of all,
When that same star that's westward from the pole
Had made its course to light that part of heaven

Where now it burns, Marcellus and myself,
The bell then beating one . . .

> (*Enter* GHOST. *He is in full armour, with*
> *visor up so that we see his pale face*)

MARCELLUS

Peace, break it off; look, there it comes again!

BERNARDO

In the same figure, like the king that's dead.

MARCELLUS

You are a scholar; speak to it, Horatio.

BERNARDO

Looks it not like the king? mark it, Horatio.

HORATIO

Most like; it harrows me with fear and wonder.

BERNARDO

It would be spoke to.

MARCELLUS

>   Question it, Horatio.

HORATIO

What are you that usurp this time of night
Together with that fair and warlike form
In which his majesty the buried king of Denmark
Did sometimes march? by heaven I charge you, speak!

MARCELLUS

It is offended.

BERNARDO

                    See, it stalks away!

HORATIO

Stay! speak, speak! I charge you speak!

                              (*Exit* GHOST)

MARCELLUS

It's gone, and will not answer.

BERNARDO

How now, Horatio! you tremble and look pale;
Is not this something more than fantasy?
What do you think of it?

HORATIO

Before my God, I never could believe this
Without the stark and solid testimony
Of my own eyes.

MARCELLUS

                    Is it not like the king?

HORATIO

As you are like yourself.
Such was the very armour he had on
When he the ambitious king of Norway slew;
So frowned he once, when, in an angry parley,
He smote the sledded Polacks on the ice.
'Tis strange.

MARCELLUS

Thus twice before, and just at this dead hour,
With martial steps has he gone by our watch.

HORATIO

I know not what to think of it for certain;
But, in the gross and scope of my opinion,
This bodes some strange eruption to our state.

MARCELLUS

Good now, sit down, and tell me, he that knows,
Why this same strict and most observant watch
That worries all the people of the land?
And why this daily casting of brass cannons,
And foreign trade for implements of war;
Why such impress of shipwrights, whose sore task
Does not divide the Sunday from the week;
What's in the offing, that this sweaty haste
Does make the night joint-labourer with the day.
Can one of you inform me?

HORATIO

That I can;
At least the whisper goes so. Our last king,
Whose image even just now appeared to us,
Was, as you know, by Fortinbras, the king of Norway,
Dared to the combat; in which our valiant Hamlet
Did slay this Fortinbras; who, by a sealed agreement,
Well ratified by law and heraldry,
Did forfeit, with his life, all those his lands
Which he possessed. Now, sir, young Fortinbras,
Of yet untempered mettle hot and full,
Has in the skirts of Norway here and there
Picked up a band of idle, lawless cutthroats—
This, to recover from us by strong hand
Those foresaid lands so by his father lost;
And this, I take it,
Is the main motive of our preparations,

The source of this our watch and the chief cause
Of this post-haste and bustle in the land.
I think ...

(Re-enter GHOST)

But soft! look, there it comes again!
I'll cross it, though it blast me. Stay, illusion!
If you have any sound, or use of voice,
Speak to me;
If there be any good thing to be done,
That may to you do ease and grace to me,
Speak to me;
If you are privy to your country's fate,
Which, luckily, foreknowing may avoid,
O, speak!
Or if, perchance, while living you have hoarded
Extorted treasure in the womb of earth,
For which, they say, you spirits often roam,
Speak of it! Stay, and speak!
(A cock crows. The GHOST *begins to retreat)*
Stop it, Marcellus.

MARCELLUS

Shall I strike at it with my halberd?

HORATIO

Do, if it will not stop.

BERNARDO

It's here!

HORATIO

It's here!
(Exit GHOST)

MARCELLUS

It's gone!
We do it wrong, being so majestical,
To offer it the show of violence;
For it is, as the air, invulnerable,
And our vain blows malicious mockery.

BERNARDO

It was about to speak, when the cock crew.

HORATIO

And then it started like a guilty thing
Upon a fearful summons. I have heard,
The cock, that is the trumpet to the morn,
Does with his lofty and shrill-sounding throat
Awake the god of day; and at his warning,
Whether in sea or fire, in earth or air,
The wandering and erring spirit hurries
To his confine; and of the truth herein
This present happening does give us proof.

MARCELLUS

It faded on the crowing of the cock.
Some say that ever when that season comes
Wherein our Saviour's birth is celebrated,
The bird of dawning sings throughout the night;
And then, they say, no spirit dares walk abroad,
The nights are wholesome, then no planets strike,
No fairy takes, nor witch has power to charm,
So hallowed and so gracious is the time.

HORATIO

So have I heard and do in part believe it.

But, look, the morn, in russet mantle clad,
Walks o'er the dew of that high eastward hill.
Break we our watch up; and, by my advice,
Let us impart what we have seen to-night
Unto young Hamlet; for, upon my life,
This spirit, dumb to us, will speak to him.
Do you consent we shall acquaint him with it,
As duty and our love for him would prompt us?

MARCELLUS

Let's do it, pray.

(*Exeunt*)

SCENE 2

A ROOM OF STATE IN THE CASTLE—*next morning.*

A flourish of trumpets. Enter CLAUDIUS, KING OF DENMARK; GERTRUDE, *the* QUEEN; PRINCE HAMLET, POLONIUS, LAERTES, VOLTEMAND, CORNELIUS, LORDS, LADIES *and* ATTENDANTS. KING *and* QUEEN *ascend to their thrones. This is a formal session of the Court. Everyone is in full dress, except* HAMLET, *who wears black.*

KING

Though yet of Hamlet our dear brother's death
The memory be green, and that it us befitted
To bear our hearts in grief, and our whole kingdom
To be contracted in one brow of woe,
Yet so far has discretion fought with nature,
That we with wisest sorrow think of him,
Together with remembrance of ourselves.
Therefore our former sister, now our queen,
The imperial jointress to this warlike state,
Have we, as 'twere with a defeated joy,
With an auspicious and a dropping eye,

With mirth in funeral, and with dirge in marriage,
In equal scale weighing delight and dole,
Taken to wife. Nor have we herein barred
Your better wisdoms, which have freely gone
With this affair along. For all, our thanks.
Now follows, that you know, young Fortinbras,
Holding a weak supposal of our worth,
Or thinking by our late dear brother's death
Our state to be disjoint and out of frame,
Deluded by the dream of his advantage,
He has not failed to pester us with message
Importing the surrender of those lands
Lost by his father, with all bonds of law,
To our most valiant brother. We have here written
To Norway, uncle of young Fortinbras—
Who, impotent and bed-rid, scarcely hears
Of this his nephew's purpose—to suppress
His further march herein. We here dispatch
You, good Cornelius, and you, Voltemand,
For bearers of this greeting to old Norway.
  (*Hands* VOLTEMAND *a scroll*)
Farewell, and let your haste commend your duty.
     (*Exeunt* VOLTEMAND *and* CORNELIUS)
And now, Laertes, what's the news with you?
You told us of some suit; what is't, Laertes?
You cannot speak of reason to the king,
And lose your plea; what would you beg, Laertes,
That shall not be my offer, not your asking?
The head is not more native to the heart,
The hand more instrumental to the mouth,
Than is the throne of Denmark to your father.
What would you have, Laertes?

[76]

LAERTES

My dread lord,
Your leave and favour to return to France,
From where though willingly I came to Denmark,
To show my duty in your coronation,
Yet now, I must confess, that duty done,
My thoughts and wishes bend again toward France.

KING

Have you your father's leave? What says Polonius?

POLONIUS

He has, my lord.
I do beseech you, give him leave to go.

KING

Take your fair hour, Laertes; time be yours,
And your best graces spend it at your will!—
But now, my nephew Hamlet, and my son . . .

HAMLET (*Aside*)

A little more than kin, and less than kind.

KING

How is it that the clouds still hang on you?

HAMLET

Not so, my lord; I am too much in the sun.

QUEEN

Good Hamlet, cast your nighted colour off,
And let your eye look like a friend on Denmark.

Do not for ever with your down-cast lids
Seek for your noble father in the dust.
You know it's common, all that lives must die,
Passing through nature to eternity.

HAMLET

Ay, madam, it is common.

QUEEN

                              If it be,
Why seems it so particular with you?

HAMLET (*Caustic and scornful*)

Seems, madam? nay, it is; I know not "seems."
It's not alone my inky cloak, good mother,
Nor customary suits of solemn black,
No, nor the tearful deluge from the eyes,
Together with all forms, modes, shows of grief,
That can denote me truly. These indeed seem,
For they are actions that a man might play;
But I have that within which passes show;
These but the trappings and the suits of woe.

KING

It's sweet and commendable in your nature, Hamlet,
To give these mourning duties to your father;
But, you must know, your father lost a father,
That father lost, lost his, and the survivor bound
In filial obligation for some term
To do obsequious sorrow. But to persevere
In obstinate condolement is a course
Of impious stubbornness; it's unmanly grief;

It shows a will most incorrect to heaven,
A heart unfortified, a mind impatient,
An understanding simple and unschooled,
A fault against the dead, a fault to nature.
We pray you, throw to earth
This unavailing woe, and think of us
As of a father; for let the world take note,
You are the most immediate to our throne,
And with no less nobility of love
Than that which dearest father bears his son
Am I inclined tow'rd you. For your intent
In going back to school in Wittenberg,
It is most contrary to our desire;
And we beseech you, bend you to remain
Here in the cheer and comfort of our eye,
Our chiefest courtier, nephew, and our son.

QUEEN

Let not your mother lose her prayers, Hamlet;
I pray you, stay with us; go not to Wittenberg.

HAMLET

I shall in all my best obey you, madam.

KING

Why, it's a loving and a fair reply;
Be as ourself in Denmark.—Madam, come;
This gentle and unforced accord of Hamlet
Sits smiling to my heart; in honour of it,
No jocund toast your king will drink to-day,
But the great cannon to the clouds shall tell,

And the king's revelry the heavens shall echo,
Re-speaking earthly thunder.—Come away.

(*Flourish of trumpets. Exeunt all but* HAMLET)

HAMLET

O, that this too too solid flesh would melt,
Thaw and dissolve itself into a dew!
Or that the Everlasting had not fixed
His canon 'gainst self-slaughter! O God! God!
How weary, stale, flat, and unprofitable
Seem to me all the uses of this world!
Fie on't! O fie! 'Tis an unweeded garden
That grows to seed; things rank and gross in nature
Possess it merely. That it should come to this!
But two months dead—nay, not so much, not two—
So excellent a king, that was to this
Hyperion to a satyr; so loving to my mother,
That he might not allow the winds of heaven
Visit her face too roughly.—Heaven and earth!
Must I remember?—Why, she would hang on him,
As if increase of appetite had grown
By what it fed on; yet, within a month—
Let me not think on't! Frailty, thy name is woman!—
A little month, or ere those shoes were old,
With which she followed my poor father's body,
Like Niobe, all tears, why she, even she—
O God! a beast that lacks the power of reason
Would have mourned longer—married with my uncle;
My father's brother, but no more like my father
Than I to Hercules. Within a month,
Ere yet the salt of most unrighteous tears
Had left the flushing in her swollen eyes,
She married. O, most wicked speed, to post

[8 0]

With such dexterity to incestuous sheets!
It is not nor it cannot come to good.
But break my heart, for I must hold my tongue!

(*Enter* HORATIO, MARCELLUS, *and* BERNARDO)

HORATIO

Hail to your lordship!

HAMLET

                      I am glad to see you . . .
Horatio!—or I do forget myself.

HORATIO

The same, my lord, and your poor servant ever.

HAMLET

Sir, my good friend; I'll change that name with you.
What brings you here from Wittenberg, Horatio?—
Marcellus!

MARCELLUS

My good lord!

HAMLET

I am very glad to see you. (*To* BERNARDO) Good even, sir.—
But what, in faith, brings you from Wittenberg?

HORATIO

A truant disposition, good my lord.

HAMLET

I would not hear your enemy say so,
Nor shall you do my ear that violence,

To make it truster of your own report
Against yourself; I know you are no truant.
But what is your affair in Elsinore?
We'll teach you to drink deep ere you depart.

HORATIO

My lord, I came to see your father's funeral.

HAMLET

I pray you, do not mock me, fellow-student;
I think it was to see my mother's wedding.

HORATIO

Indeed, my lord, it followed hard upon.

HAMLET

Thrift, thrift, Horatio! the funeral baked meats
Did coldly furnish forth the marriage tables.
Would I had met my direst foe in heaven
Ere ever I had seen that day, Horatio!
My father!—methinks I see my father.

HORATIO

O where, my lord?

HAMLET

In my mind's eye, Horatio.

HORATIO

I saw him once; he was a goodly king.

HAMLET

He was a man; take him for all in all,
I shall not look upon his like again.

HORATIO

My lord, I think I saw him yesternight.

HAMLET

Saw whom?

HORATIO

My lord, the king your father.

HAMLET

The king my father?

HORATIO

Pray, temper your amazement for a while
With an attentive ear, till I relate,
Upon the witness of these gentlemen,
This marvel to you.

HAMLET

For God's love, let me hear.

HORATIO

Two nights together had these gentlemen,
Marcellus and Bernardo, on their watch
In the dead void and middle of the night
Been thus encountered. A figure like your father,
Completely armed, from head to foot,
Appears before them and with solemn march
Goes slow and stately by them. Thrice he walked
By their oppressed and terror-stricken eyes
Within his truncheon's length; while they, distilled
Almost to jelly with the act of fear,
Stand dumb, and speak not to him. This to me
In dreadful secrecy they did impart;

[83]

And I with them the third night kept the watch;
Where, as they had delivered, both in time,
Form of the thing, each word made true and good,
The apparition comes. I knew your father;
These hands are not more like.

HAMLET

But where was this?

MARCELLUS

My lord, upon the platform where we watched.

HAMLET

Did you not speak to it?

HORATIO

My lord, I did;
But answer made it none. Yet once I thought
It turned its head, as if about to speak,
But even then the morning cock crew loud,
And at the sound it shrunk in haste away
And vanished from our sight.

HAMLET

It's very strange.

HORATIO

As I do live, my honoured lord, it's true;
And we did think it writ down in our duty
To let you know of it.

HAMLET

Indeed, indeed, sirs, but this troubles me.
Hold you the watch to-night?

[8 4]

MARCELLUS and BERNARDO

We do, my lord.

HAMLET

Armed, you say?

MARCELLUS

Armed, my lord.

HAMLET

From top to toe?

BERNARDO

My lord, from head to foot.

HAMLET

Then saw you not his face?

HORATIO

O, yes, my lord; he wore his visor up.

HAMLET

What, looked he frowningly?

HORATIO

A countenance more in sorrow than in anger.

HAMLET

Pale, or red?

HORATIO

Nay, very pale.

HAMLET

And fixed his eyes upon you?

[85]

HORATIO

Most constantly.

HAMLET

I would I had been there.

HORATIO

It would have much amazed you.

HAMLET

Very like, very like. . . . Stayed it long?

HORATIO

While one with moderate haste might count a hundred.

MARCELLUS

Longer.

BERNARDO

Longer.

HORATIO

Not when I saw it.

HAMLET

His beard was grizzled? no?

HORATIO

It was, as I have seen it in his life,
A sable silvered.

HAMLET

I will watch to-night;
Perchance 'twill walk again.

[86]

HORATIO

I warrant it will.

HAMLET

If it assumes my noble father's person,
I'll speak to it, though hell itself should gape
And bid me hold my peace. I pray you all,
If you have hitherto concealed this sight,
Let it be tenable in your silence still;
And whatsoever else shall hap'n to-night,
Give it an understanding, but no tongue.
I will requite your loves. So, fare you well;
Upon the platform, 'twixt eleven and twelve,
I'll visit you.

ALL

Our duty to your honour.

HAMLET

Your love, as mine to you. Farewell.

(*Exeunt all but* HAMLET)

My father's spirit—in arms! All is not well;
I fear some foul play. Would the night were come!
Till then sit still, my soul. Foul deeds will rise,
Though all the earth o'erwhelm them, to men's eyes.

(*Exit*)

SCENE 3

A ROOM IN POLONIUS' HOUSE—*that afternoon.*
Enter LAERTES *and* OPHELIA.

LAERTES

My necessaries are embarked; farewell;
And, sister, let me hear from you.

OPHELIA

D'you doubt that?

LAERTES

For Hamlet, and the trifling of his favour,
Hold it a fashion, and a toy in blood;
A violet in the youth of primy nature,
Forward, not permanent, sweet, not lasting;
The perfume and suppliance of a minute;
No more.

OPHELIA

No more but so?

LAERTES

Think it no more.

Perhaps he loves you now,
And now no soil nor cunning does besmirch
The virtue of his will; but you must fear,

His greatness weighed, his will is not his own;
For he himself is subject to his birth.
He may not, as unvalued persons do,
Carve for himself, for on his choice depends
The safety and health of this whole state.
Then weigh what loss your honour may sustain,
If with too credulous ear you heed his songs,
Or lose your heart, or your chaste treasure open
To his unmastered importunity.
Fear it, Ophelia, fear it, my dear sister,
And keep yourself restrained in your affection,
Out of the shot and danger of desire.
The chariest maid is prodigal enough,
If she unmask her beauty to the moon.
The canker galls the blossoms of the spring
Too often ere their buds be fully blown,
And in the morn and liquid dew of youth
Contagious blastments are most imminent.
Be wary then; best safety lies in fear.

OPHELIA

I shall the effect of this good lesson keep
As watchman to my heart. But, good my brother,
Do not, as some ungracious pastors do,
Show me the steep and thorny way to heaven,
While, like a puffed and reckless libertine,
Himself the primrose path of dalliance treads,
And heeds not his own counsel.

LAERTES

        Fear that not!
I stay too long; but here my father comes.

(Enter POLONIUS*)*

Occasion smiles upon a second leave.

[89]

POLONIUS

Still here, Laertes? aboard, aboard, for shame!
The wind sits in the shoulder of your sail,
And you are waited for. My blessing with you!
And these few precepts in your memory
Look you engrave. Give your thoughts no tongue,
Nor any unproportioned thought his act.
Be you familiar, but by no means vulgar. *common*
Those friends you have, and their adoption tried,
Grapple them to your soul with hoops of steel;
But do not dull your palm with entertainment
Of each new-hatched, unfledged companion. Beware
Of entrance to a quarrel, but being in,
Bear't that the opposed may beware of you.
Give every man your ear, but few your voice;
Take men's opinions, but reserve your judgement.
Costly your habit as your purse can buy,
But not expressed in fancy; rich, not gaudy;
For the apparel oft proclaims the man.
Neither a borrower, nor a lender be;
For loan oft loses both itself and friend,
And borrowing dulls the edge of husbandry.
This above all: to your own self be true;
And it must follow, as the night the day,
You cannot then be false to any man.
Farewell; my blessing season this in you!

LAERTES

Most humbly do I take my leave, my lord.

POLONIUS

The time invites you; go, your servants wait.

LAERTES

Farewell, Ophelia, and remember well
What I have said to you.

OPHELIA

It's in my memory locked,
And you yourself shall keep the key of it.

LAERTES (*Embracing her*)

Farewell.   (*Exit*)

POLONIUS

What is't, Ophelia, he has said to you?

OPHELIA

So please you, something touching the Lord Hamlet.

POLONIUS

Marry, well bethought!
It's told me, he has very oft of late
Given private time to you, and you yourself
Have of your audience been most free and bounteous.
If it be so—as so it's put to me,
And that in way of caution—I must tell you,
You do not understand yourself so clearly
As it behooves my daughter and your honour.
What is between you? give me up the truth.

OPHELIA

He has, my lord, of late made many tenders
Of his affection to me.

POLONIUS

Affection? pooh! You speak like a green girl,
Unsifted in such perilous circumstance.
Do you believe his tenders, as you call them?

OPHELIA

I do not know, my lord, what I should think.

POLONIUS

Marry, I will teach you. Think yourself a baby,
That you have tak'n these tenders for true pay,
Which are not sterling. Tender yourself more dearly,
Or—not to crack the wind of the poor phrase,
Running it thus—you'll tender me a fool.

OPHELIA

My lord, he has expressed his urgent love
In honourable fashion.

POLONIUS

Ay, fashion you may call it; go to, go to.

OPHELIA

And has given countenance to his speech, my lord,
With almost all the holy vows of heaven.

POLONIUS

Ay, snares to capture woodcocks! I do know,
When the blood burns, how prodigal the soul
Lends the tongue vows. These blazes, daughter,
Giving more light than heat, extinct in both
Even in their promise, as it is a-making,
You must not take for fire. For Lord Hamlet,

Believe so much in him, that he is young,
And with a larger tether may he walk
Then may be given you. In short, Ophelia,
Do not believe his vows; for they are brokers,
Breathing like sanctified and pious bawds,
The better to beguile. This is for all:
I would not, in plain terms, from this time forth
Have you so slander any moment's leisure
As to give words or talk with the Lord Hamlet.
Look to't, I charge you; come your ways.

OPHELIA (*Controlling her tears*)

I shall obey, my lord.

(*Exeunt*)

SCENE 4

The platform on the battlements—*that night.*
Enter HAMLET, HORATIO, *and* MARCELLUS.

HAMLET

The air bites shrewdly; it is very cold.

HORATIO

It is a nipping and an eager air.

HAMLET

What hour now?

HORATIO

I think it lacks of twelve.

MARCELLUS

No, it is struck.

HORATIO

Indeed? I heard it not. It then draws near the time,
Wherein the spirit held his wont to walk.
(*A flourish of trumpets, and ordnance shot* O. S.)
What does this mean, my lord?

HAMLET

The king sits up to-night in drunken revel;
And, as he drains his draughts of Rhenish wine,

[94]

The kettle-drum and trumpet thus bray out
The triumph of his toast.

HORATIO

Is it a custom?

HAMLET

Ay, marry, it is;
But to my mind, though I am native here
And to the manner born, it is a custom
More honoured in the breach than the observance.
This heavy-headed revel east and west
Makes us defamed and scorned by other nations.
They call us drunkards, and with swinish phrase
Soil our good title; and indeed it takes
From our achievements, though performed at height,
The pith and marrow of our reputation.
So, oft it chances in particular men,
That for some vicious mole of nature in them,
As in their birth—wherein they are not guilty,
Since nature cannot choose its origin—
That these men,
Carrying, I say, the stamp of one defect,
Their other virtues—be they as pure as grace,
As infinite as man may ever reach—
Shall in the public judgement take corruption
From that particular fault.

(*Enter* GHOST)

HORATIO

Look, my lord, it comes!

HAMLET

Angels and ministers of grace defend us!
Be thou a spirit of health or goblin damned,

[95]

Bring with thee airs from heaven or blasts from hell,
Be thy intents wicked or charitable,
Thou com'st in such a questionable shape
That I will speak to thee. I'll call thee Hamlet,
King, father, Royal Dane. O, answer me!
Let me not burst in ignorance, but tell
Whý thy cánonized bones, hearsed in death,
Have burst their cerements? why the sepulchre,
Wherein we saw thee quietly interred,
Has oped his ponderous and marble jaws,
To cast thee up again? What may this mean,
That thou, dead corpse, again in armour clad,
Revisit'st thus the glimpses of the moon,
Making night hideous, and us, fools of nature,
So horridly to shake our disposition
With thoughts beyond the reaches of our souls?
Say, why is this? wherefore? what should we do?

(GHOST *beckons* HAMLET)

HORATIO

It beckons you to go away with it,
As if it some impartment did desire
To you alone.

MARCELLUS

            Look with what courteous action
It waves you to a more secluded ground;
But do not go with it.

HORATIO

                No, by no means.

[96]

HAMLET

It will not speak; then I will follow it.

HORATIO

Do not, my lord.

HAMLET

                    Why, what should be the fear?
I do not set my life at a pin's fee;
And for my soul, what can it do to that,
Being a thing immortal as itself?
It waves me forth again; I'll follow it.

HORATIO

What if it tempt you toward the flood, my lord,
Or to the dreadful summit of the cliff,
That beetles o'er its base into the sea,
And there assume some other horrible form,
Which might deprive you of your sovereign reason,
And draw you into madness?

HAMLET

                    It waves me still.—
Go on; I'll follow thee.

MARCELLUS

You shall not go, my lord.

HAMLET

                    Hold off your hands.

HORATIO

Be ruled; you shall not go.

HAMLET

My fate cries out,
And makes each petty artery in this body
As hardy as the Nemean lion's nerve.

(GHOST *beckons*)

Still am I called. Unhand me, gentlemen—
(*Breaking from them and drawing his sword*)
By heaven, I'll make a ghost of him that holds me!
I say, away!—Go on, I'll follow thee.

(*Exeunt* GHOST *and* HAMLET)

HORATIO

He waxes desperate with imagination.

MARCELLUS

Let's follow; it's not fit thus to obey him.

HORATIO

Have after. To what issue will this come?

MARCELLUS

Something is rotten in the state of Denmark.

(*Exeunt*)

SCENE 5

ANOTHER PART OF THE PLATFORM ON THE BATTLEMENTS—
directly following.

Enter GHOST *and* HAMLET.

HAMLET

Where wilt thou lead me? speak, I'll go no further.

GHOST

Mark me.

HAMLET

I will.

GHOST

My hour is almost come,
When I to sulphurous and tormenting flames
Must render up myself.

HAMLET

Alas, poor ghost!

GHOST

Pity me not, but lend thy serious hearing
To what I shall unfold.

[99]
[001]

42375

HAMLET

Speak; I am bound to hear.

GHOST

So art thou to revenge, when thou shalt hear.

HAMLET

What?

GHOST

I am thy father's spirit;
Doomed for a certain term to walk the night,
And for the day confined to fast in fires,
Till the foul crimes done in my days on earth
Are burnt and purged away. But that I am forbidden
To tell the secrets of my prison-house,
I could a tale unfold whose lightest word
Would harrow up thy soul, freeze thy young blood,
Make thy two eyes, like stars, start from their spheres,
Thy smoothly interwoven locks to part,
And each particular hair to stand on end,
Like quills upon the fretful porcupine.
But this eternal blazon must not be
To ears of flesh and blood. O, listen! listen!
If thou didst ever thy dear father love. . . .

HAMLET

Oh God!

GHOST

Revenge his foul and most unnatural murder.

HAMLET

Murder?

GHOST

Murder most foul, as at the best it is;
But this most foul, strange, and unnatural.

HAMLET

Haste me to know't, that I, with wings as swift
As meditation or the thoughts of love,
May sweep to my revenge.

GHOST

I find thee apt.

Now, Hamlet, hear:
'Tis given out, that, sleeping in my orchard,
A serpent stung me; so the whole ear of Denmark
Is by a false reporting of my death
Rankly abused; but know, thou noble youth,
The serpent that did sting thy father's life
Now wears his crown.

HAMLET

O my prophetic soul!

My uncle!

GHOST

Ay, that incestuous, that adulterous beast,
With witchcraft of his wit, with traitorous gifts—
O wicked wit and gifts, that have the power
So to seduce!—won to his shameful lust
The will of my most seeming-virtuous queen.
O Hamlet, what a falling-off was there,
From me, whose love was of that dignity
That it went hand in hand even with the vow
I made to her in marriage, and to decline
Upon a wretch whose natural gifts were poor

Compared to mine!
But virtue, as it never will be moved,
Though lewdness court it in a shape of heaven,
So lust, though to a radiant angel linked,
Will sate itself in a celestial bed
And prey on garbage.
But, soft, methinks I scent the morning air;
Brief let me be. Sleeping within my orchard,
My custom always in the afternoon,
On my unguarded hour thy uncle stole,
With juice of cursed hebenon in a vial,
And in the porches of my ears did pour
The leperous distilment, whose effect
Holds such an enmity with blood of man
That swift as quicksilver it courses through
The natural gates and alleys of the body.
Thus was I, sleeping, by a brother's hand
Of life, of crown, of queen, at once dispatched;
Cut off even in the blossoms of my sin,
Unhouseled, unanointed, unprepared;
No reckoning made, but sent to my account
With all my imperfections on my head.

HAMLET

O horrible! Oh, horrible! most horrible!

GHOST

If thou hast feelings in thee, bear it not ;
Let not the royal bed of Denmark be
A couch for lust and damnéd incest.
But, howsoever thou pursuest this act,
Taint not thy mind, nor let thy soul contrive
Against thy mother aught. Leave her to heaven,

And to those thorns that in her bosom lodge
To prick and sting her. Fare thee well at once!
The glow-worm shows the morning to be near,
And 'gins to pale his ineffectual fire.
Adieu, adieu, adieu! remember me.   (*Exit*)

HAMLET

O all you host of heaven! O earth! what else?
And shall I couple hell? . . . Hold, hold, my heart!
And you, my sinews, grow not instant old,
But bear me stiffly up. Remember thee?
Ay, thou poor ghost, while memory holds a seat
        (*Indicating his head*)
In this distracted globe. Remember thee?
Yea, from the pages of my memory
I'll wipe away all trivial fond records,
All saws of books, all forms, all pressures past,
That youth and observation copied there,
And thy commandment all alone shall live
Within the book and volume of my brain,
Unmixed with baser matter. Yes, by heaven!
O most pernicious woman!
O villain, villain! smiling, damnéd villain!
Ay, meet it is for me to set it down
That one may smile, and smile, and be a villain;
At least I'm sure it may be so in Denmark.
So, uncle, there you are! Now to my word—
It is: "Adieu, adieu! remember me."
I've sworn it.

MARCELLUS (*O. S.*)

My lord!

HORATIO (O. S.)

My lord!

MARCELLUS (O. S.)

Lord Hamlet!

HORATIO (O. S.)

Heaven secure him!

HAMLET

So be it!

HORATIO (O. S.)

Hillo, ho, ho, my lord!

HAMLET

Hillo, ho, ho, boy! come, bird, come.
(Enter HORATIO and MARCELLUS)

MARCELLUS

How is't, my noble lord?

HORATIO

What news, my lord?

HAMLET

O, wonderful!

HORATIO

Good my lord, tell it.

HAMLET

No; you will reveal it.

HORATIO

Not I, my lord, by heaven!

MARCELLUS

Nor I, my lord.

HAMLET

What say you, then, would ever man conceive it? . . .
But you'll be secret?

HORATIO and MARCELLUS

Ay, by heaven, my lord.

HAMLET

There's ne'er a villain dwelling in all Denmark . . .
    (*He is about to say: "Like my uncle Claudius," but
    checks himself*)
Who's not an arrant knave.

HORATIO

There needs no ghost, my lord, come from the grave
To tell us this.

HAMLET

Why, right! You're in the right!
And so, without more words or ceremony,
I hold it fit that we shake hands and part;
You, as your business and desire shall point you—
For every man has business and desire,
Such as it is—and for my own poor part,
Look you, I will go pray.

HORATIO

These are but wild and whirling words, my lord.

HAMLET

I'm sorry they offend you, heartily;
Yes, faith, heartily.
      (*Turns and walks a few steps away from them*)

HORATIO (*Follows* HAMLET)

There's no offence, my lord.

HAMLET

      (*To* HORATIO, *out of earshot of* MARCELLUS)
Yes, by Saint Patrick, but there is, Horatio,
And much offence too. Touching this vision here,
It is an honest ghost, that let me tell you.
For your desire to know what is between us,
O'ermaster't as you may.
      (*To both* MARCELLUS *and* HORATIO)
                And now, good friends,
As you are friends, scholars, and soldiers,
Give me one poor request.

HORATIO

What is't, my lord? we will.

HAMLET

Never make known what you have seen to-night.

HORATIO and MARCELLUS

My lord, we will not.

HAMLET

Nay, but swear it.

HORATIO

In faith,

My lord, not I.

MARCELLUS

Nor I, my lord, in faith.

HAMLET (*Drawing his sword*)

Upon my sword.

MARCELLUS

We have sworn, my lord, already.

HAMLET

Indeed, upon my sword, indeed.

GHOST (*Beneath*)

Swear.

HAMLET

Ah, ha, boy! say you so? still there, old gaffer?
Come on, you hear this fellow underground,
Consent to swear.

HORATIO

Propose the oath, my lord.

HAMLET

Never to speak of this that you have *seen*,
Swear by my sword.
(*They lay their hands on the hilt of* HAMLET'S *sword*)

GHOST (*Beneath*)

Swear.

HAMLET

Hic et ubique? then we'll shift our ground.
Come hither, gentlemen,
And lay your hands again upon my sword.
Never to speak of this that you have *heard*,
Swear by my sword.

GHOST (*Beneath*)

Swear.
    (*They swear again*)

HAMLET

Well said, old mole! You dig through earth most fast!
A worthy miner!—Once more remove, good friends.

HORATIO

O day and night, but this is wondrous strange!

HAMLET

And therefore as to a stranger give it welcome.
There are more things in heaven and earth, Horatio,
Than are dreamt of in your philosophy.
But come;
Here, as before, never, so help you mercy,
However strange or odd I bear myself—
As I perchance hereafter shall think meet
To put an antic disposition on—
That you, at such times seeing me, never shall,
With arms thus folded, or this kind of head-shake,
Or by pronouncing of some doubtful phrase,
As "Well, well, we know," or "If we cared to speak,"
Or such ambiguous hinting, to imply

That you know aught of me—this not to do,
So grace and mercy at your great need help you,
Swear.

GHOST (*Beneath*)

Swear.

(*They swear for the third time*)

HAMLET

(*Aside*) Rest, rest, perturbéd spirit!—So, gentlemen,
With all my love I do commend me to you;
And what so poor a man as Hamlet is
May do t' express his love and friendship to you,
God willing, shall not lack. Let us go in together;
And still your fingers on your lips, I pray.—
The time is out of joint. O curséd spite,
That ever I was born to set it right!—
Nay, come, let's go together.

(*Exeunt*)

A C T   I I

A C T II

S C E N E 1

A ROOM IN POLONIUS' HOUSE—*about seven weeks later*.
Enter POLONIUS *and* REYNALDO.

POLONIUS
Give Laertes this money and these notes, Reynaldo.

REYNALDO
I will, my lord.

POLONIUS
You shall do marvellous wisely, good Reynaldo,
Before you visit him, to make inquiry
Of his behaviour.

REYNALDO
My lord, I did intend it.

POLONIUS
Marry, well said; very well said. Look you, sir,
Inquire me first what Danes there are in Paris,

[1 1 3]

And how, and who, what means, and where they live;
What company, at what expense; and finding
That they do know my son, approach more closely,
As thus, "I know his father and his friends,
And in part him." Do you mark this, Reynaldo?

REYNALDO

Ay, very well, my lord.

POLONIUS

"And in part him; but,"—you may say—"not well.
But if it's who I mean, he's very wild,
Addicted so and so,"—and there put on him
What forgeries you please; marry, none so rank
As may dishonour him—take heed of that—
But, sir, such wanton, wild, and usual slips
As are companions noted and most known
To youth and liberty.

REYNALDO

As gaming, my lord.

POLONIUS

Ay, or drinking, fencing, swearing, quarrelling,
Whoring—you may go so far.

REYNALDO

My lord, that would dishonour him.

POLONIUS

Faith, no; as you may breathe his faults so quaintly
That they may seem the taints of liberty,

The flash and outbreak of a fiery mind,
A savageness in young and untamed blood.

REYNALDO

But, my good lord . . .

POLONIUS

Wherefore should you do this?

REYNALDO

Ay, my lord.

POLONIUS

Because he answers then: "I know the gentleman;
I saw him yesterday, or t'other day,
Or then, or then, with such, or such; and, as you say,
There was he gaming, drinking"; or perchance,
"I saw him enter such a house of sale,"
That is to say, a brothel, or so forth.
See you now;
Your bait of falsehood hooks this carp of truth;
And thus do we of wisdom and of foresight
By indirections find directions out.
You have me, have you not?

REYNALDO

My lord, I have.

POLONIUS

God be with you; fare you well.

REYNALDO

Good my lord!

POLONIUS

Observe his inclinations for yourself.

REYNALDO

I shall, my lord.

POLONIUS

And let him ply his music.

REYNALDO

Well, my lord.

POLONIUS

Farewell!

(*Exit* REYNALDO.
Enter OPHELIA)

How now, Ophelia! what's the matter?

OPHELIA

Oh, my lord, my lord, I've been so frightened!

POLONIUS

With what, in the name of God?

OPHELIA

My lord, as I was sewing in my room,
Lord Hamlet—with his doublet all unbraced,
No hat upon his head, his stockings fouled,
Pale as his shirt, his knees knocking each other,
And with a look so piteous in expression
As if he had been loosed out of hell
To speak of horrors—he comes before me.

[116]

POLONIUS

Mad for your love?

OPHELIA

My lord, I do not know,
But truly I do fear it.

POLONIUS

What said he?

OPHELIA

He took me by the wrist, and held me hard;
Then goes he to the length of all his arm,
And with his other hand thus o'er his brow,
He falls to such perusal of my face
As if he'd draw it. Long stayed he so.
At last, a little shaking of my arm,
And thrice his head thus waving up and down,
He raised a sigh so piteous and profound
As it did seem to shatter all his bulk,
And end his being; that done, he lets me go;
And, with his head over his shoulder turned,
He seemed to find his way without his eyes,
For out of doors he went without their help,
And to the last he kept their light on me.

POLONIUS

Come, go with me; I will go seek the king.
This is the very madness of hot love,
Whose flaming violénce destroys itself
And leads the will to desperate undertakings.
What, have you given him any hard words of late?

OPHELIA

No, my good lord; but, as you did command,
I did repel his letters, and denied
His access to me.

POLONIUS

                    That has made him mad.
I am sorry that with better heed and judgement
I had not reckoned him. I feared he did but trifle,
And meant to wreck you.
Come, go we to the king; this must be known.
Come.

                                        (*Exeunt*)

SCENE 2

A ROOM IN THE CASTLE—*shortly following.*
Flourish of trumpets. Enter KING, QUEEN, ROSENCRANTZ, GUIL-
DENSTERN, *and* ATTENDANTS.

KING

Welcome, dear Rosencrantz and Guildenstern!
Besides our dearest wish to see you both,
The need we have to use you did provoke
Our hasty summons. You must have heard some news
Of Hamlet's transformation—so call it,
Since neither the exterior nor the inward man
Resembles what he was. What it should be,
More than his father's death, that thus has put him
So much from the understanding of himself,
I cannot dream of. I entreat you both,
That, being from young days brought up with him,
And since so neighboured to his youth and nature,
You will consent to stay here in our court
Some little time; so by your company
To draw him on to pleasures, and to gather,
So much as from occasions you may glean,
If something, now unknown to us, afflicts him,
That, opened, lies within our remedy.

QUEEN

Good gentlemen, he has much talked of you;

[119]

And I am sure there are not two men living
To whom he more adheres. If it will please you
To show us so much kindness and good will
As to expend your time with us awhile,
And help us to achieve our fervent hope,
Your visitation shall receive such thanks
As fits a king's remembrance.

ROSENCRANTZ

                        Both your majesties
Might, by the sovereign power you have o'er us,
Put your dread pleasures more into command
Than to entreaty.

GUILDENSTERN

                        But we both obey,
And here give up ourselves, in fullest measure,
To lay our service freely at your feet,
To be commanded.

KING

Thanks, Rosencrantz and noble Guildenstern.

QUEEN

Thanks, Guildenstern and noble Rosencrantz.
And I beseech you instantly to visit
My poor, distracted son. Go, some of you,
And take these gentlemen at once to Hamlet.

GUILDENSTERN

May heavens make our presence and our efforts
Pleasant and helpful to him!

QUEEN

Ay, amen!

(*Exeunt* ROSENCRANTZ, GUILDENSTERN,
and some ATTENDANTS.

Enter POLONIUS)

POLONIUS (*To the* KING)

The ambassadors from Norway, my good lord,
Have joyfully returned.

KING

You've always been the father of good news.

POLONIUS

Have I, my lord? Assure you, my good liege,
I hold my duty, as I hold my soul,
Both to my God and to my gracious king;
And I do think—or else this brain of mine
Hunts not the trail of policy so sure
As it has used to do—that I have found
The very cause of Hamlet's lunacy.

KING

O, speak of that! That do I long to hear.

POLONIUS

Give first admittance to the ambassadors,
And let my news be the dessert to that great feast.

KING

Do grace to them yourself, and bring them in.

(*Exit* POLONIUS)

He tells me, my dear Gertrude, he has found
The cause and source of all your son's distemper.

[1 2 1]

QUEEN

I fear it is no other but the main:
His father's death, and our o'erhasty marriage.

KING

Well, we shall sift him.

(*Re-enter* POLONIUS, *with*
VOLTEMAND *and* CORNELIUS)
Welcome, my good friends!
Say, Voltemand, what from our brother Norway?

VOLTEMAND

Most fair return of greetings and good wishes.
Upon your word, he sent out to suppress
His nephew's levies, which to him appeared
To be a preparation 'gainst the Polack,
But better looked into, he truly found
It was against your highness; whereat grieved,
That so his sickness, age and impotence
Was falsely served, at once sends out arrests
On Fortinbras; which he, in brief, obeys;
Receives rebuke from Norway; and at last
Makes vow before his uncle never more
To take up arms against your majesty.
Whereon old Norway, overcome with joy,
Gives him three thousand crowns in annual fee,
And his commission to employ those soldiers,
So levied as before, against the Polack;
With an entreaty, herein further shown,
        (*Giving a paper*)
That it might please you to give quiet pass
Through your dominions for this enterprise.

KING

We like it well;
And at a more appropriate time we'll read,
Answer, and think upon this business.
Meantime, we thank you for your well-done labour.
Go to your rest; at night we'll feast together.
Most welcome home!

(*Exeunt* VOLTEMAND, CORNELIUS *and* ATTENDANTS)

POLONIUS

This business is well ended.
My liege, and madam, to expostulate
What majesty should be, what duty is,
Why day is day, night night, and time is time,
Were nothing but to waste night, day, and time.
Therefore, since brevity is the soul of wit,
I will be brief. Your noble son is mad.
Mad call I it, for, to define true madness,
What is't but to be nothing else but mad?
But let that go.

QUEEN

More matter, with less art.

POLONIUS

Madam, I swear I use no art at all.
That he is mad, 'tis true; 'tis true 'tis pity;
And pity 'tis 'tis true. A foolish figure!
But farewell it, for I will use no art.
Mad let us grant him then; and now remains
That we find out the cause of this effect,
Or rather say, the cause of this defect,
For this effect defective comes by cause.

[1 2 3]

Thus it remains, and the remainder thus.
Perpend.
I have a daughter—have while she is mine—
Who, in her duty and obedience, mark,
Has given me this. Now gather, and surmise.
    (*Reads*)
"To the celestial and my soul's idol, the most beautiful
  Ophelia, . . ."
"In her excellent white bosom, these" . . . etc . . .

QUEEN

This came to her from Hamlet?

POLONIUS

Good madam, wait awhile; I will be faithful.
    (*Reads*)
        "Doubt you the stars are fire,
          Doubt that the sun does move,
          Doubt truth to be a liar,
          But never doubt I love.
O dear Ophelia, I am bad at poetry; I have not the art to rhyme
my woes; but that I love you best, O most best, believe it. Adieu.
                Yours evermore, most dear lady,
while this body of mine still lives,

                    Hamlet."
This in obedience has my daughter shown me;
And more besides, has his solicitations,
As they fell out by time, by means, and place,
All given to mine ear.

KING

                  But how has she
Received his love?

POLONIUS

What do you think of me?

KING

As of a man faithful and honourable.

POLONIUS

I would fain prove so. But what might you think,
When I had seen this hot love on the wing—
As I perceived it, I must tell you that,
Before my daughter told me—what might you,
Or my dear majesty your queen here, think,
If I had looked on it with idle sight;
What might you think? No, I went straight to work,
And my young daughter thus I did address:
"Lord Hamlet is a prince, he's far above you;
This must not be." And then I prescripts gave her,
That she should lock herself from his approach,
Admit no messengers, receive no tokens.
Which done, she took the fruits of my advice;
And he, repulsed—a short tale to make—
Fell into a sadness, then into a fast,
Thence to a watch, thence into a weakness,
Thence to a lightness, and, by this declension,
Into the madness wherein now he raves,
And we all mourn for.

KING

Do you think it's this?

QUEEN

It may be, very likely.

[125]

POLONIUS

Has there been such a time—I'd like to know that—
That I have positively said " 'Tis so,"
When it proved otherwise?

KING

                                Not that I know.

POLONIUS

(*Pointing to his head and shoulder*)
Take this from this, if this be otherwise.
If circumstances lead me, I will find
Where truth is hid, though it were hid indeed
Within the very centre of the earth.

KING

How may we try it further?

POLONIUS

You know, sometimes he walks for hours together
Here in the lobby.

QUEEN

                                So he does indeed.

POLONIUS

At such a time I'll loose my daughter to him.
Be you and I behind a drapery then;
Watch the encounter; if he loves her not,
And is not from his reason fall'n thereon,
Let me be no assistant for a state,
But keep a farm and carters.

KING

We will try it.

QUEEN

But look where sadly the poor dear comes reading.

POLONIUS

Away, I do beseech you, both away;
I'll board him presently.

(*Exeunt* KING, QUEEN, *and* ATTENDANTS.
Enter HAMLET, *reading*)

How does my good Lord Hamlet?

HAMLET

Well, God have mercy.

POLONIUS

Do you know me, my lord?

HAMLET

Excellent well; you are a fishmonger.

POLONIUS

Not I, my lord.

HAMLET

Then I would you were so honest a man.

POLONIUS

Honest, my lord?

[127]

HAMLET

Ay, sir; to be honest, as this world goes, is to be one man picked out of ten thousand.

POLONIUS

That's very true, my lord.

HAMLET

For if the sun breeds maggots in a dead dog, being a god kissing carrion . . . Have you a daughter?

POLONIUS

I have, my lord.

HAMLET

Let her not walk in the sun. Conception is a blessing, but not as your daughter may conceive. Friend, look to it.

POLONIUS

What say you by that? (*Aside*) Still harping on my daughter; yet he knew me not at first; he said I was a fishmonger. He is far gone, far gone; and truly in my youth I suffered much extremity for love; very near this. I'll speak to him again.—What do you read, my lord?

HAMLET

Words, words, words.

POLONIUS

What is the matter, my lord?

HAMLET

Between whom?

POLONIUS

I mean, the matter that you read, my lord.

HAMLET

Slanders, sir; for the satirical rogue says here that old men have gray beards, that their faces are wrinkled, their eyes purging thick amber and plumtree gum, and that they have a plentiful lack of wit, together with most weak hams. All of which, sir, though I most powerfully and potently believe, yet I hold it not gentlemanly to have it thus set down; for you yourself, sir, would be old as I am, if, like a crab, you could go backward.

POLONIUS (*Aside*)

Though this be madness, yet there is method in it.—Will you walk out of the air, my lord?

HAMLET

Into my grave?

POLONIUS

Indeed, that's out of the air. (*Aside*) How pregnant sometimes his replies are! I will leave him, and suddenly contrive the means of a meeting between him and my daughter.—My honourable lord, I will most humbly take my leave of you.

HAMLET

You cannot, sir, take from me any thing that I will more willingly part with—except my life, except my life, except my life.

POLONIUS

Fare you well, my lord. (*Starts to leave*)

HAMLET

These tedious old fools!

(*Enter* ROSENCRANTZ *and* GUILDENSTERN)

POLONIUS

You go to seek the Lord Hamlet; there he is.

ROSENCRANTZ (*To* POLONIUS)

God save you, sir!

(*Exit* POLONIUS)

GUILDENSTERN

My honoured lord!

ROSENCRANTZ

My most dear lord!

HAMLET

My excellent good friends! How do you, Guildenstern?
Ah, Rosencrantz! Good lads, how do you both?

ROSENCRANTZ

As the average children of the earth.

GUILDENSTERN

Happy, in that we are not over-happy;
On Fortune's cap we are not the very button.

HAMLET

Nor the soles of her shoe?

ROSENCRANTZ

Neither, my lord.

HAMLET

Then you live about her waist, or in the middle of her favours?

GUILDENSTERN

Faith, her privates we.

HAMLET

In the secret parts of Fortune? Oh, most true;
She is a strumpet. What's the news?

ROSENCRANTZ

None, my lord, but that the world's grown honest.

HAMLET

Then is doomsday near. But your news is not true. Let me question more in particular: what have you, my good friends, deserved at the hands of Fortune, that she sends you to prison here?

GUILDENSTERN

Prison, my lord?

HAMLET

Denmark's a prison.

ROSENCRANTZ

Then is the world one.

HAMLET

A goodly one; in which there are many confines, wards and dungeons; Denmark being one of the worst.

ROSENCRANTZ

We think not so, my lord.

HAMLET

Why, then it's none to you; for there is nothing either good or bad, but thinking makes it so. To me it is a prison.

ROSENCRANTZ

Why, then your ambition makes it one; it's too narrow for your mind.

HAMLET

O God, I could be bounded in a nut-shell, and count myself a king of infinite space, were it not that I have bad dreams.

GUILDENSTERN

Which dreams, indeed, are ambition; for the very substance of the ambitious is merely the shadow of a dream.

HAMLET

A dream itself is but a shadow.

ROSENCRANTZ

Truly, and I hold ambition of so airy and light a quality that it is but a shadow's shadow.

HAMLET

By faith, I cannot reason! . . . But, in the beaten way of friendship, what are you doing in Elsinore?

ROSENCRANTZ

To visit you, my lord; no other occasion.

HAMLET

Beggar that I am, I am even poor in thanks; but I thank you. . . . Were you not sent for? Did you come of your own accord? Is it a free visit? Come, deal justly with me. Come, come; nay, speak.

GUILDENSTERN

What should we say, my lord?

HAMLET

Why, anything, but to the purpose. You were sent for; and there is a kind of confession in your looks, which your natures have not craft enough to conceal. I know the good king and queen have sent for you.

ROSENCRANTZ

To what end, my lord?

HAMLET

That you must teach me. But let me conjure you, by the rights of our fellowship, by the consonancy of our youth, by the obligation of our ever-preserved love, be honest and direct with me, whether you were sent for, or not.

ROSENCRANTZ (*To* GUILDENSTERN)

What do you say?

HAMLET

Nay, then, I have an eye on you. If you love me, do not hold off.

GUILDENSTERN

My lord, we were sent for.

HAMLET

I will tell you why; so my anticipation shall prevent your disclosure, and your secrecy to the king and queen moult no feather. I have of late—but wherefore I know not—lost all my mirth, forgone all custom of exercises; and indeed it goes so heavily with my disposition, that this goodly frame, the earth, seems to me a sterile promontory; this most excellent canopy, the air, look you, this brave overhanging firmament, this majestical roof fretted with golden fire, why, it appears no other thing to me than a foul and pestilent congregation of vapours. . . . What a piece of work is man! how noble in reason! how infinite in faculties! in form and moving, how express and admirable! in action, how like an angel! in apprehension, how like a god! the beauty of the world! the paragon of animals! And yet, to me, what is this quintessence of dust? Man delights me not—no, nor woman neither, though by your smiling you seem to say so.

ROSENCRANTZ

My lord, there was no such stuff in my thoughts.

HAMLET

Why did you laugh then, when I said "man delights me not"?

ROSENCRANTZ

To think, my lord, if you delight not in man, what meagre reception the players shall receive from you. We passed them on the way; and they are coming here to offer you service.

HAMLET

He that plays the king shall be welcome; his majesty shall have tribute of me, the adventurous knight shall use his foil and target, the lover shall not sigh gratis. What players are they?

ROSENCRANTZ

Even those you used to take such delight in, the tragedians of the city.

HAMLET

How does it happen that they are touring? Do they hold the same esteem as they did when I was in the city? Are they as popular?

ROSENCRANTZ

No, indeed, they are not.

HAMLET

How come? Have they grown rusty?

ROSENCRANTZ

No, they are as good as ever; but there are now in the city companies of children, little boy-actors, who are most extravagantly applauded; these are now the fashion.

HAMLET

Is it possible? . . . And the boys win the day?

ROSENCRANTZ

Ay, that they do, my lord.

HAMLET

It is not very strange; for my uncle is king of Denmark, and those that would make faces at him while my father lived, give twenty, fifty, a hundred ducats a-piece for his picture. By God, there is something in this more than natural, if philosophy could find it out.

(*Flourish of trumpets O. S.*)

GUILDENSTERN

There are the players.

HAMLET

Gentlemen, you are welcome to Elsinore. You are welcome; but my uncle-father and aunt-mother are deceived.

GUILDENSTERN

In what, my dear lord?

HAMLET

I am but mad north-north-west; when the wind is southerly, I know a hawk from a heron.

(Re-enter POLONIUS*)*

POLONIUS

Well be with you, gentlemen!

HAMLET

Listen, Guildenstern, and you too,—at each ear a hearer—that great baby, you see there, is not yet out of his swaddling clothes.

ROSENCRANTZ

They say, an old man is twice a child.

HAMLET

I will prophesy he comes to tell me of the players; mark it.—You say right, sir, on Monday morning, it was so indeed.

POLONIUS

My lord, I have news to tell you.

HAMLET

My lord, I have news to tell you: when Roscius was an actor in Rome, . . .

POLONIUS

The actors have come here, my lord.

HAMLET

Buz, buz!

POLONIUS

Upon my honour . . .

HAMLET

Then came each actor on his ass. . . .

POLONIUS

The best actors in the world, either for tragedy, comedy, history,
pastoral, pastoral-comical, historical-pastoral, tragical-historical,
tragical-comical-historical-pastoral. Seneca cannot be too heavy,
nor Plautus too light. . . .

HAMLET

O Jephthah, judge of Israel, what a treasure you had!

POLONIUS

What treasure had he, my lord?

HAMLET

Why,

"One fair daughter, and no more,
The which he lovéd passing well."

POLONIUS (*Aside*)

Still on my daughter.

HAMLET

Am I not in the right, old Jephthah?

[137]

POLONIUS

If you call me Jephthah, my lord, I have a daughter that I love passing well.

HAMLET

Nay, that follows not.

POLONIUS

What follows, then, my lord?

HAMLET

Why, . . .

(Enter four or five PLAYERS)

You are welcome, masters; welcome, all. I am glad to see you well. Welcome, good friends.—O, my old friend! Your face is bearded since I saw you last.—Masters, you are all welcome. We'll have a speech straight away. Come, give us a taste of your quality; come, a passionate speech.

FIRST PLAYER

What speech, my good lord?

HAMLET

I heard you speak a speech once, but it was never acted; or, if it was, not more than once; because the play, I remember, did not please the millions; it was caviar to the general public; but it was—as I thought, and others, whose judgements in such matters topped mine—an excellent play, well digested in the scenes, set down with as much simplicity as skill. I remember, one said there were no spicy bits in the lines to make the matter savoury. One speech in it I chiefly loved; it was Aeneas' tale to Dido, and especially, where he speaks of Priam's slaughter. If it live in your memory, begin at this line; let me see, let me see:

"The rugged Pyrrhus, like the Hyrcanian tiger," . . .
  It's not so; it begins with "Pyrrhus."
"The rugged Pyrrhus—he whose mighty shield,
  Black as his purpose, did the night resemble
  When he lay hidden in the ominous horse—
  With eyes like carbuncles old Priam seeks."
So, proceed.

POLONIUS

By God, my lord, well spoken; with good accent and good discretion.

FIRST PLAYER

             "And then he finds him
Striking too short at Greeks; his antique sword,
Rebellious to his arm, lies where it falls,
Repugnant to command. Unequal matched,
Pyrrhus at Priam drives; in rage strikes wide;
But with the whiff and wind of his dread sword
The unnerved father falls. Pyrrhus stood still;
Did nothing.
But as we often see, before some storm,
A silence in the heavens, the clouds stand still,
The bold winds speechless, and the earth below
As hush as death, and then the dreadful thunder
Does rend the air; so after Pyrrhus' pause
His risen vengeance sets him anew to work;
And never did the Cyclops' hammers fall
On Mars's armour, forged for proof eternal,
With less remorse than Pyrrhus' bleeding sword
Now falls on Priam.
Out, out, thou strumpet Fortune!"

POLONIUS

This is too long.

HAMLET

It shall to the barber's with your beard.—Pray you, say on—he goes for a jig or a tale of bawdry, or he sleeps—say on; come to Hecuba.

FIRST PLAYER

"But who, O, who had seen the muffled queen
Run barefoot up and down, threatening the flames
With blinding tears; a rag upon that head
Where late the diadem stood; and for a robe,
A blanket, in the alarm of fear caught up—
Who this had seen, with tongue in venom steeped
Would have rebelled 'gainst Fortune's cruel power.
But if the gods themselves did see her then,
When she saw Pyrrhus make malicious sport
In mincing with his sword her husband's limbs,
The instant burst of clamour that she made—
Unless things mortal move them not at all—
Would have made weep the burning eyes of heaven,
And stirred the gods to passion!"

POLONIUS

Look, if he has not turned his colour, and has tears in his eyes.—Pray you, no more.

HAMLET

It's well; I'll have you speak the rest of this soon.—Good my lord, will you see the players well lodged? Do you hear, let them be well treated; for they are the abstracts and brief chronicles of the time. It would be better for you to have a bad epitaph after your death than their ill report while you live.

POLONIUS

My lord, I will use them according to their desert.

HAMLET

Good God, man, much better! Use every man after his desert, and who shall escape whipping? Use them after your own honour and dignity; the less they deserve, the more merit is in your bounty. Take them in.

POLONIUS

Come, sirs.

HAMLET

Follow him, friends; we'll hear a play tomorrow.

(*Exit* POLONIUS *with all the* PLAYERS *but the* FIRST, *whom* HAMLET *detains*)

Hear me, old friend; can you play "The Murder of Gonzago"?

FIRST PLAYER

Ay, my lord.

HAMLET

We'll have it tomorrow night. You could, if needed, learn a speech of some dozen or sixteen lines, which I would set down and insert in it, could you not?

FIRST PLAYER

Ay, my lord.

HAMLET

Very well. Follow that lord; and look you do not mock him.

(*Exit* FIRST PLAYER)

My good friends, I'll leave you till night. You are welcome to Elsinore.

ROSENCRANTZ

Good my lord.

HAMLET

Ay, so, God be with you!

(*Exeunt* ROSENCRANTZ *and* GUILDENSTERN)

Now I am alone.

O, what a rogue and peasant slave am I!
Is it not monstrous that this player here,
But in a fiction, in a dream of passion,
Could force his soul so to his own conceit
That from her working all his visage wanned,
Tears in his eyes, distraction in his aspect,
A broken voice, and his whole function fitting
In forms to his design? and all for nothing!
For Hecuba!
What's Hecuba to him, or he to Hecuba,
That he should weep for her? What would he do,
Had he the motive and the cue for passion
That I have? He would drown the stage with tears
And cleave the public ear with horrid speech,
Make mad the guilty, and appal the free,
Confound the ignorant, and amaze indeed
The very faculties of eyes and ears.
Yet I,
A dull and muddy-mettled rascal, peak,

Like John-a-dreams, unpregnant of my cause,
And can say nothing; no, not for a king,
Upon whose crown, and wife, and most dear life,
A damned defeat was made. Am I a coward?
Who calls me villain? breaks my pate across?
Tweaks me by the nose? gives me the lie in the throat,
As deep as to the lungs? who does me this, ha?
'Swounds, I should take it; for it cannot be
But I am pigeon-livered and lack gall
To make oppression bitter, or ere this
I should have fatted all the region vultures
With this slave's offal. Bloody, bawdy villain!
Remorseless, treacherous, lecherous, vicious villain!
O, vengeance!
Why, what an ass am I. This is most brave,
That I, the son of a dear father murdered,
Prompted to my revenge by heaven and hell,
Must, like a whore, unpack my heart with words,
And fall a-cursing, like a very drab,
A scullion!
Fie upon't! foh! About, my brain! Hum! I have heard
That guilty creatures, sitting at a play,
Have by the very cunning of the scene
Been struck so to the soul, that presently
They have proclaimed their malefactions;
For murder, though it has no tongue, will speak
With most miraculous organ. I'll have these players
Play something like the murder of my father
Before my uncle; I'll observe his looks;
I'll probe him to the quick; if he but blench,
I know my course. The spirit that I have seen
May be a devil; and the devil has power

To assume a pleasing shape; yea, and perhaps
Out of my weakness and my melancholy,
As he is very potent with such spirits,
Abuses me to damn me. I'll have grounds
More relevant than this. The play's the thing
Wherein I'll catch the conscience of the king.

(*Exit*)

A C T   III

ACT III

SCENE 1

A ROOM IN THE CASTLE—*next day.*
Enter KING, QUEEN, POLONIUS (*with a book in his hand*),
OPHELIA, ROSENCRANTZ *and* GUILDENSTERN.

KING

And can you by no drift of circumstance
Get from him why he puts on this confusion,
Grating so harshly all his days of quiet
With turbulent and dangerous lunacy?

ROSENCRANTZ

He does confess he feels himself distracted,
But from what cause he will by no means speak.

GUILDENSTERN

Nor do we find him forward to be sounded,
But with a crafty madness keeps aloof,
When we would bring him on to some confession
Of his true state.

QUEEN

Did he receive you well?

ROSENCRANTZ

Most like a gentleman.

GUILDENSTERN

But with much forcing of his disposition.

ROSENCRANTZ

Niggard of question, but of our demands
Most free in his reply.

QUEEN

Did you entice him
To any pastime?

ROSENCRANTZ

Madam, it so fell out that certain players
We passed by on the way. Of these we told him,
And there did seem in him a kind of joy
To hear of it. They are about the court,
And, as I think, they have already orders
This night to play before him.

POLONIUS

'Tis most true;
And he beseeched me to entreat your majesties
To hear and see the matter.

KING

With all my heart; and it does much content me
To hear him so inclined.

Good gentlemen, give him a further edge,
And drive his purpose on to these delights.

ROSENCRANTZ

We shall, my lord.

(*Exeunt* ROSENCRANTZ *and* GUILDENSTERN)

KING

Sweet Gertrude, leave us too;
We secretly have sent for Hamlet hither,
That he, as 'twere by accident, may here
Confront Ophelia.
Her father and myself—lawful spies—
Will so conceal ourselves that, seeing unseen,
We may of their encounter frankly judge,
And gather from him, as he is behaved,
If't be the affliction of his love, or no,
That thus he suffers for.

QUEEN

I shall obey you.
And for your part, Ophelia, I do wish
That your good beauty be the happy cause
Of Hamlet's wildness; so shall I hope your virtue
Will bring him to his wonted way again,
To both your honours.

OPHELIA

Madam, I wish it may.

(*Exit* QUEEN)

POLONIUS

Ophelia, walk you here.—My liege, so please you,
We will conceal ourselves.

(*To* OPHELIA, *as he gives her the book*)

                  Pretend to read this book;
This show of exercise will justify
Your loneliness. We are oft to blame in this—
'Tis so well proved—that with devotion's visage
And pious action we do sugar over
The devil himself.

KING (*Aside*)

              O, it's too true!
How smart a lash that speech does give my conscience!
The harlot's cheek, beautified with plastering art,
Is not more ugly to the thing that helps it
Than is my deed to my most painted words.
O heavy burden!

POLONIUS

I hear him coming; let's withdraw, my lord.
      (*They conceal themselves behind the tapestry.* OPHELIA
      begins her walk, pretending to read the book. She
      slowly exits S. R. to re-enter later)

                    (*Enter* HAMLET *S. L.*)

HAMLET

To be, or not to be—that is the question;
Whether 'tis nobler in the mind to suffer
The slings and arrows of outrageous fortune,
Or to take arms against a sea of troubles,
And by opposing end them. To die—to sleep—
No more; and by a sleep to say we end
The heart-ache and the thousand natural shocks
That flesh is heir to. 'Tis a consummation
Devoutly to be wished. To die—to sleep.

To sleep—perchance to dream! ay, there's the rub;
For in that sleep of death what dreams may come,
When we have shuffled off this mortal coil,
Must give us pause—thére's the motive
That makes us cling to life's calamities.
For who would bear the whips and scorns of time,
Th' oppressor's wrong, the proud man's contumely,
The pangs of despised love, the law's delay,
The insolence of office, and the spurns
That patient merit from the unworthy takes,
When he himself might his own ending make
With a mere dagger? Who would these burdens bear,
To grunt and sweat under a weary life,
But that the dread of something after death—
The undiscovered country from whose bounds
No traveller returns—puzzles the will,
And makes us rather bear those ills we have
Than fly to others that we know not of?
Thus conscience does make cowards of us all;
And thus the native hue of resolution
Is sicklied o'er with the pale cast of thought,
And enterprises of great pitch and moment
With this regard their currents turn awry,
And lose the name of action . . .
                    (OPHELIA *re-enters S. R., pretending to read her book*)
                              Soft you now,
The fair Ophelia!—Nymph, in thy orisons
Be all my sins remembered.

OPHELIA

(From here on till HAMLET's *first "Farewell"* OPHELIA *is
trying to put on a performance. She is bad at it—help-*

less, embarrassed, and conscious of the hidden eaves-
droppers)
                                          Good my lord,
How does your honour for this many a day?

HAMLET

I humbly thank you; well, well, well.

OPHELIA

My lord, I have remembrances of yours,
That I have longed long to re-deliver;
I pray you, now receive them.
          (*She offers* HAMLET *a small velvet pouch containing his*
          gifts)

HAMLET

                                          No, not I;
I never gave you aught.

OPHELIA

My honoured lord, you know right well you did;
And with them words of so sweet breath composed
As made the things more rich. Their perfume lost,
Take these again; for to the noble mind
Rich gifts wax poor when givers prove unkind.
There, my lord.

HAMLET

          (*Shocked by her preposterous "act"*)
Ha, ha! are you honest?

OPHELIA

My lord?

HAMLET

Are you fair?

OPHELIA

What means your lordship?

HAMLET

(*Speaking as he would to a misled child*)
That if you be honest and fair, your honesty should admit no bargaining with your beauty.

OPHELIA

(*Keeping up her pretence*)
Could beauty, my lord, have better commerce than with honesty?

HAMLET (*Bitterly*)

Ay, truly; for the power of beauty will sooner transform honesty from what it is to a bawd, than the force of honesty can translate beauty into its likeness. This was once a paradox, but now the time gives it proof. I did love you once.

OPHELIA

Indeed, my lord, you made me believe so.

HAMLET

You should not have believed me; for virtue cannot so inoculate our old stock as to transform it. I loved you not.

[153]

OPHELIA

I was the more deceived.

HAMLET

(*Again as to a child, with throbbing tenderness and sorrow*)

Go to a nunnery; why would you be a breeder of sinners? I am myself fairly honest, but yet I could accuse me of such things that it were better my mother had not borne me. I am very proud, revengeful, ambitious; with more offences at my beck than I have thoughts to put them in, imagination to give them shape, or time to act them in. What should such fellows as I do, crawling between earth and heaven? We are arrant knaves all; believe none of us. Go your way to a nunnery.

(*He puts his arms around* OPHELIA *and holds her close in a gesture of love and protection. She yields at first, then suddenly turns her head toward the tapestry and, alarmed, guiltily breaks away from* HAMLET. *It is obvious that they are being spied upon*)

Where's your father?

OPHELIA

At home, my lord.

HAMLET

(*Hurt and infuriated by this brazen lie, lashes out, making sure he is heard by the spies, as well as by* OPHELIA)

Let the doors be shut upon him, that he may play the fool no where but in his own house. Farewell.

OPHELIA

O, help him, you sweet heavens!

HAMLET

If you do marry, I'll give you this plague for your dowry: be
you as chaste as ice, as pure as snow, you shall not escape cal-
umny. Go to a nunnery, go; farewell. Or, if you must marry,
marry a fool; for wise men know well enough what monsters
you make of them. To a nunnery, go; and quickly too. Farewell.

OPHELIA

O heavenly powers, restore him!

HAMLET

I have heard of your paintings too, well enough. God has given
you one face, and you make yourselves another; you jig, you
amble, and you lisp; and nickname God's creatures, and pretend
your wantonness is your ignorance. Go to, I'll have no more
of it; it has made me mad. I say, we will have no more marriages;
those that are married already, all but one, shall live; the rest
shall keep as they are. To a nunnery, go.

(Exit)

OPHELIA

O, what a noble mind is here o'erthrown!
The courtier's, scholar's, soldier's, eye, tongue, sword,
Th' expectancy and rose of the fair state,
The glass of fashion, and the mould of form,
Th' observed of all observers—quite, quite down!
And I, of ladies most deject and wretched,
That sucked the honey of his music vows,
Now see that noble and most sovereign reason,
Like sweet bells jangled, out of tune and harsh;
That unmatched form and feature of blown youth
Blasted with madness! Oh!—woe is me,

T' have seen what I have seen, see what I see!
>   (*She dissolves into tears*)
>   (*Re-enter* KING *and* POLONIUS)

KING

Love? his emotions do not tend that way;
Nor what he spoke, though it lacked form a little,
Was not like madness. There's something in his soul,
O'er which his melancholy sits on brood;
And I suspect the hatch and the disclosure
Will be some danger—which to prevent,
I have in quick determination
Thus set it down: he shall with speed to England,
For the demand of our neglected tribute.
Haply the seas, and countries different,
With variable objects, shall expel
This something-settled matter in his heart,
Whereon his brains still beating puts him thus
From fashion of himself. What think you of it?

POLONIUS

It shall do well; but yet do I believe
The origin and commencement of his grief
Sprung from neglected love.—How now, Ophelia!
You need not tell us what Lord Hamlet said;
We heard it all.
>   (OPHELIA, *covering her face with her hands in distress*
>   *and in shame, runs out*)
>   My lord, do as you please;
But, if you hold it fit, after the play,
Let his queen mother all alone entreat him
To show his grief. Let her be blunt with him;
And I'll be placed, so please you, in the ear

Of all their conference. If she solve him not,
To England send him; or confine him where
Your wisdom best shall think.

KING

                    It shall be so.
Madness in great ones must not unwatched go.

                                 (*Exeunt*)

SCENE 2

Enter HAMLET *and* PLAYERS.

HAMLET

Speak the speech, I pray you, as I pronounced it to you, trippingly on the tongue. But if you mouth it, as many of your players do, I would as well the town-crier spoke my lines. Nor do not saw the air too much with your hand, thus, but use all gently; for in the very torrent, tempest, and, as I may say, whirlwind of your passion, you must acquire and beget a temperance that may give it smoothness. O, it offends me to the soul to hear a robustious periwig-pated ham tear a passion to tatters, to very rags, to split the ears of the groundlings, who for the most part are capable of nothing but inexplicable dumb-shows and noise. I would have such a ham whipped. It out-herods Herod. Pray you, avoid it.

FIRST PLAYER

I warrant your honour.

HAMLET

Be not too tame neither, but let your own discretion be your tutor. Suit the action to the word, the word to the action; with this special observance, that you do not overstep the modesty of nature; for any thing so overdone is away from the purpose of acting, whose end, both at the first and now, was and is, to hold, as it were, the mirror up to nature; to show virtue its own feature, scorn its own image, and the very age and body of the time its form and pressures. Now this overdone, or come short of, though it make the unskillful laugh, cannot but make the judicious grieve, the opinion of one of whom must in your allowance overweigh a whole theatre of others. O, there be players that I have seen play, and heard others praise, and that highly, that—not to speak it profanely—neither having the accent of Christians nor the gait of Christian, pagan, nor man, have so strutted and bellowed, that I have thought some of nature's apprentices had made them, and not made them well, they imitated humanity so abominably.

First Player

I hope we have reformed that fairly well with us, sir.

Hamlet

O, reform it altogether. And let your comedians speak no more than is set down for them. For there are some of them that will themselves laugh, to set on a number of half-witted spectators to laugh too, though in the meantime some necessary question of the play is to be considered. That's villainous, and shows a most pitiful ambition in the fool that uses it. Go, make you ready.

(*Exeunt* PLAYERS)

Horatio!

(*Enter* HORATIO)

Horatio

Here, dear lord, at your service.

HAMLET

Horatio, you are even as just a man
As ever I have met with.

HORATIO

O, my dear lord!

HAMLET

Nay, do not think I flatter;
For what advancement may I hope from you,
Who have no revenue but your good spirits
To feed and clothe you? Why should the poor be flattered?
No, let the candied tongue lick foolish pomp,
And crook the ready hinges of the knee
Where gain may follow fawning. Do you hear?
Since my free soul was mistress of her choice,
And could of men distinguish, her election
Has sealed you for herself. For you have been
As one, in suffering all, that suffers nothing;
A man that fortune's buffets and rewards
Have taken with equal thanks; and blest are those
Whose blood and judgement are so well commingled,
That they are not a pipe for Fortune's finger
To sound what stop she please. Give me that man
That is not passion's slave, and I will wear him
In my heart's core, ay, in my heart of heart,
As I do you. But that's enough of that!
There is a play to-night before the king.
One scene of it comes near the circumstance
Which I have told you of my father's death;
I pray you, when you see that act afoot,
Even with the very comment of your soul
Observe my uncle. If his occulted guilt

Does not itself unravel in one speech,
It is a damnéd ghost that we have seen,
And my imaginations are as foul
As Vulcan's smithy. Give him heedful note;
For I my eyes will rivet to his face,
And after we will both our judgements join.

HORATIO

Well, my lord.
> (*Flourish of trumpets and kettle-drums O. S.*)

HAMLET

They are coming to the play. I must act mad.
Get you a place.
> (*Danish march. Enter* KING, QUEEN, POLONIUS, OPHELIA, ROSENCRANTZ, GUILDENSTERN, *and other* LORDS *attendant, with the* GUARD *carrying torches. The following scene is in essence a deadly duel between* HAMLET *and the* KING. HAMLET *is the aggressor; like a persistent wasp, he stings and probes the* KING. *His ultimate purpose is the* KING's *confession.*)

KING

How fares our nephew Hamlet?

HAMLET

Excellent, in faith; on the chameleon's dish: I eat the air, promise-crammed. You cannot feed capons so.

KING

I make nothing of this answer, Hamlet. These words are no reply to mine.

[161]

HAMLET

No, nor to mine now. (*To* POLONIUS) My lord, you played once in the university, you say?

POLONIUS

That I did, my lord; and was accounted a good actor.

HAMLET

And what did you enact?

POLONIUS

I did enact Julius Caesar; I was killed in the Capitol; Brutus killed me.

HAMLET

It was a brute part of him to kill so capital a calf there.—Are the players ready?

ROSENCRANTZ

Ay, my lord; they wait upon your pleasure.

QUEEN

Come hither, my dear Hamlet, sit by me.

HAMLET (*Referring to* OPHELIA)

No, good mother, here's metal more attractive.

POLONIUS (*To the* KING)

O, ho! do you mark that?
> (POLONIUS *stays close to* HAMLET *to eavesdrop.* HAMLET *knows it, and his following sentences are meant more for* POLONIUS *than* OPHELIA)

HAMLET

Lady, shall I lie in your lap?

OPHELIA

No, my lord.

HAMLET

I mean, my head upon your lap?

OPHELIA

Ay, my lord.

HAMLET

Do you think I meant unseemly matters?

OPHELIA

I think nothing, my lord.

HAMLET

That's a fair thought
> (*Turning away from* OPHELIA *straight to* POLONIUS
> *standing at his heels:*)
>> to lie between maid's legs.

OPHELIA

> (*Who has not heard the second half of* HAMLET'*s sentence*)
What is, my lord?

HAMLET (*Back to* OPHELIA)

Nothing.

OPHELIA

You are merry, my lord.

HAMLET

Who, I?

OPHELIA

Ay, my lord.

HAMLET

(From now on every speech he addresses to OPHELIA *is
for the ears of the* KING *and the* QUEEN)
O God, your only jester. What should a man do but be merry?
for, look you, how cheerfully my mother looks, and my father
died within these two hours.

OPHELIA

Nay, it's twice two months, my lord.

HAMLET

So long? Nay then, let the devil wear black, for I'll have a
suit of sables. O heavens! die two months ago, and not forgotten
yet? Then there's hope a great man's memory may outlive his
life half a year.

> *Trumpets sound. The Dumb-Show enters:*
> *Enter a* KING *and a* QUEEN *very lovingly; the* QUEEN *embracing him and he her. She kneels, and makes a show
> of affection for him. He takes her up, and declines his
> head upon her neck. He lays himself down upon a
> bank of flowers. She, seeing him asleep, leaves him. Enters a fellow, takes off the* KING'S *crown, kisses it, pours
> poison in the* KING'S *ears, and exits. The* QUEEN *returns,
> finds the* KING *dead, and makes passionate action. The*

POISONER, *with some two or three* MUTES, *comes in
again, seeming to lament with her. The dead body is
carried away. The* POISONER *woos the* QUEEN *with gifts;
she seems loath and unwilling awhile, but in the end
accepts his love.* (*Exeunt*)
(*Throughout the above* HAMLET's *eyes are riveted to*
CLAUDIUS *and* GERTRUDE. CLAUDIUS *watches the Dumb-
Show with a hard, expressionless face.*)

OPHELIA

What does this mean, my lord?

HAMLET

(*More to the* KING *than to* OPHELIA)
Marry, this is skulking mischief; it means mischief.

OPHELIA

Perhaps this show conveys the argument of the play.
(*Enter* PROLOGUE)

HAMLET (*At the* KING)

We shall know by this fellow. The players cannot keep a secret;
they'll tell all.

OPHELIA

Will he tell us what this show meant?

HAMLET (*At the* KING)

Ay, or any show that you'll show him. If you won't be ashamed
to show, he won't be ashamed to tell you what it means.

OPHELIA

You are wicked, you are wicked. I'll watch the play.

[165]

PROLOGUE

For us, and for our tragedy,
Here stooping to your clemency,
We beg your hearing patiently.   (*Exit*)

HAMLET

Is this a prologue, or the posy of a ring?

OPHELIA

It's brief, my lord.

HAMLET

As woman's love.

(*Enter two* PLAYERS, *a* KING *and a* QUEEN)

PLAYER KING

Full twenty times has Phoebus' cart gone round
Neptune's salt seas and Tellus' orbéd ground,
And twenty dozen moons with borrowed sheen
About the world have times twelve twenties been,
Since love our hearts, and Hymen did our hands,
Unite commutual in most sacred bands.

PLAYER QUEEN

So many journeys may the sun and moon
Make us again count o'er ere love be done!
But, woe is me! you are so sick of late,
So far from cheer and from your former state.

PLAYER KING

Faith, I must leave you, love, and shortly too;
My faculties their functions cease to do;

[166]

And you shall live in this fair world behind,
Honoured, beloved; and haply one as kind
For husband shall you. . . .

PLAYER QUEEN

O, confound the rest!
Such love must needs be treason in my breast.
In second husband let me be accurst!
None wed the second but who killed the first.

HAMLET (*To* KING CLAUDIUS)

Wormwood, wormwood!

PLAYER QUEEN

The interests that second marriage move
Are base pursuits of gain, but none of love.
A second time I kill my husband dead,
When second husband kisses me in bed.

PLAYER KING

I do believe you think what now you speak,
But what we do determine oft we break.
For 'tis a question left us yet to prove,
Whether love leads fortune, or else fortune love.
The great man down, you see his favourites flee;
The poor advanced makes friend of enemy.
So think you will no second husband wed,
But die your thoughts when your first lord is dead.

PLAYER QUEEN

Nor earth to me give food, nor heaven light!
Sport and repose lock from me day and night!
To desperation turn my trust and hope!

A hermit's fare in prison be my scope!
Both here and hence pursue me lasting strife,
If, once a widow, ever I be wife!

HAMLET (*To* CLAUDIUS *and* GERTRUDE)

If she should break it now!

PLAYER KING

'Tis deeply sworn. Sweet, leave me here awhile;
My spirits grow dull, and fain I would beguile
The tedious day with sleep.   (*He sleeps*)

PLAYER QUEEN

Sleep rock thy brain;
And never come mischance between us twain!   (*Exit*)

HAMLET (*To* GERTRUDE)

Madam, how do you like this play?

QUEEN

The lady does protest too much, methinks.

HAMLET

O, but she'll keep her word.

KING

Have you heard the argument? Is there no offence in it?

HAMLET

No, no; they do but jest, poison in jest; no offence in the world.

KING

What do you call the play?

HAMLET

The Mouse-trap. Marry, how? Figuratively. This play is the image of a murder done in Vienna. Gonzago is the duke's name; his wife, Baptista. You shall see right away; it's a knavish piece of work; but what of that? your majesty and we who have guiltless souls, it touches us not—let the guilty wince, we who are innocent are not troubled.

(*Enter* LUCIANUS)

This is one Lucianus, nephew to the king.

OPHELIA

You are as good as a chorus, my lord.

HAMLET

I could interpret between you and your love, if I could see you dallying.

OPHELIA

Still better, and worse.

HAMLET

So you must take your husbands. (*To* LUCIANUS) Begin, murderer! Pox! stop making your damnable faces, and begin! Come —"the croaking raven does bellow for revenge."

LUCIANUS

Thoughts black, hands apt, drugs fit, and time agreeing;
All things conspiring, and no creature seeing;
Thou mixture rank, of midnight weeds collected,
With deadly curse thrice blasted, thrice infected,
Thy natural magic and dire property
On wholesome life unleash immediately.

(*Pours the poison into the sleeper's ear*)

[169]

HAMLET (*To* KING CLAUDIUS)

He poisons him in the garden for his estate; his name's Gonzago;
the story is extant, and written in very choice Italian; you shall
see at once how the murderer gets the love of Gonzago's wife.

(*The* KING *stands up. His face is ashen*)

OPHELIA

The king rises!

HAMLET (*To the* KING)

What, frightened with false fire?

QUEEN

How fares my lord?

POLONIUS

Stop the play.

KING (*On the verge of fainting*)

Give me some light! Away! ...

ALL

Lights, lights, lights!

(*Exeunt all but* HAMLET *and* HORATIO)

HAMLET (*Jubilant*)

> "Why, let the stricken deer go weep,
>   The hart ungalléd play;
> For some must watch, while some must sleep:
>   Thus runs the world away."

Would not this show, sir, that—if my fortune ever turn
Turk on me—I could earn a good salary as an actor?

HORATIO

A small salary.

HAMLET

O no, a fat one.

> For you do know, O Damon dear,
> This realm dismantled was
> Of Jove himself; and now reigns here
> A very, very—peacock.

HORATIO

You might have rhymed.

HAMLET

O good Horatio, I'll take the ghost's word for a thousand pounds.
Did you perceive?

HORATIO

Very well, my lord.

HAMLET

Upon the talk of the poisoning?

HORATIO

I did very well note him.

HAMLET

Ah, ha! Come, some music! come, the flutes!

> For if the king like not the comedy,
> Why then, belike, he likes it not, perdy.

Come, some music!

(*Re-enter* ROSENCRANTZ *and* GUILDENSTERN)

[1 7 1]

GUILDENSTERN

Good my lord, grant me a word with you.

HAMLET

Sir, a whole history.

GUILDENSTERN

The king, sir. . .

HAMLET

Ay, sir, what of him?

GUILDENSTERN

Is in his retirement exceedingly distempered.

HAMLET

With drink, sir?

GUILDENSTERN

No, my lord, rather with choler.

HAMLET

Your wisdom would show itself more richer to report this to the doctor; for, for me to put him to his purgation would perhaps plunge him into far more choler.

GUILDENSTERN

Good my lord, put your discourse into some frame and do not start so wildly from my affair.

HAMLET

I am tame, sir; pronounce.

GUILDENSTERN

The queen, your mother, in most great affliction of spirit, has sent me to you.

HAMLET

You are welcome.

GUILDENSTERN

Nay, good my lord, this courtesy is not of the right breed. If it shall please you to make me a wholesome answer, I will do your mother's commandment; if not, your pardon and my return shall be the end of my business.

HAMLET

Sir, I cannot.

GUILDENSTERN

What, my lord?

HAMLET

Make you a wholesome answer; my wit's diseased. But, sir, such answer as I can make, you shall command; or rather, as you say, my mother. Therefore no more, but to the matter! My mother, you say...

(GUILDENSTERN, *flushed with resentment, steps back*)

ROSENCRANTZ

Then thus she says: your behavior has struck her into amazement and wonder.

HAMLET

O wonderful son, that can so astonish a mother! But is there no sequel at the heels of this mother's wonder? Impart.

ROSENCRANTZ

She desires to speak with you in her room, before you go to bed.

HAMLET

We shall obey, were she ten times our mother. Have you any further trade with us?

ROSENCRANTZ

My lord, you once did love me.

HAMLET

So I do still, (*Referring to the fingers of his hand*)
                    by these pickers and stealers.

ROSENCRANTZ

Good my lord, what is the cause of your distemper? you do surely bar the door upon your own liberty, if you deny your griefs to your friend.

HAMLET

Sir, I lack advancement.

ROSENCRANTZ

How can that be, when you have the voice of the king himself for your succession in Denmark?

HAMLET

Ay, sir, but "While the grass grows,"—the proverb is somewhat musty.

(*Re-enter* PLAYERS *with flutes*)

O, the flutes! let me see one.

(Takes a flute from one of the PLAYERS *and dismisses them
with a gesture—Exeunt* PLAYERS.
Turning to GUILDENSTERN *and* ROSENCRANTZ)
Now, to have done with
you—why do you go about to the windward side of me, as if you
would drive me into a trap?

GUILDENSTERN

O, my lord, if my duty makes me too bold, then my love is too
unmannerly.

HAMLET

I do not well understand that. Will you play upon this pipe?

GUILDENSTERN

My lord, I cannot.

HAMLET

I pray you.

GUILDENSTERN

Believe me, I cannot.

HAMLET

I do beseech you.

GUILDENSTERN

I know no touch of it, my lord.

HAMLET

It's as easy as lying. Govern these stops with your fingers and
thumb, give it breath with your mouth, and it will utter most
eloquent music. Look you, these are the stops.

GUILDENSTERN

But these I cannot command to any utterance of harmony; I have not the skill.

HAMLET

Why, look you now, how unworthy a thing you make of me! You would play upon me; you would seem to know my stops; you would pluck out the heart of my mystery; you would sound me from my lowest note to the top of my compass—and there is much music, excellent voice, in this little organ; yet you cannot make it speak. 'Sblood, do you think I am easier to be played on than a pipe? Call me what instrument you will, though you can fret me, you cannot play upon me.

(*Re-enter* POLONIUS)

God bless you, sir!

POLONIUS

My lord, the queen would speak with you, and that at once.

HAMLET

Do you see yonder cloud that's almost in shape of a camel?

POLONIUS

By the mass, and 'tis like a camel, indeed.

HAMLET

Methinks it is like a weasel.

POLONIUS

It is backed like a weasel.

HAMLET

Or like a whale?

POLONIUS

Very like a whale.

HAMLET

Then I will come to my mother immediately. (*Aside*)
They fool me to the top of my bent.—I will come immediately.

POLONIUS

I will say so.

(*Exit* POLONIUS)

HAMLET

"Immediately" is easily said. Leave me, friends.

(*Exeunt all but* HAMLET)

It's now the very witching time of night,
When churchyards yawn, and hell itself breathes out
Contagion to this world. Now could I drink hot blood,
And do such bitter business as the day
Would quake to look on. Soft! now to my mother.
O heart, lose not your nature; let not ever
The soul of Nero enter this firm bosom;
Let me be cruel, not unnatural.
I will speak daggers to her, but use none;
My tongue and soul in this be hypocrites;
However by my words she may be rent,
To give them seals never, my soul, consent!

(*Exit*)

SCENE 3

A ROOM IN THE CASTLE—*directly following.*
               Enter KING, ROSENCRANTZ, *and* GUILDENSTERN.

KING

I like him not, nor stands it safe with us
To let his madness range. Therefore prepare you;
I your commission will forthwith dispatch,
And he to England shall along with you.
The terms of our estate may not endure
Hazard so near us as does hourly grow
Out of his lunacies.

GUILDENSTERN

         We will prepare ourselves.
Most holy and religious fear it is
To keep those many many bodies safe
That live and feed upon your majesty.

ROSENCRANTZ

The king dies not alone, but, like a gulf,
Does draw what's near him with him.

KING

Get ready, pray you, for this speedy voyage;
For we will fetters put upon this danger,
Which now goes too free-footed.

GUILDENSTERN

We will hasten.
(*Exeunt* ROSENCRANTZ *and* GUILDENSTERN.
Enter POLONIUS)

POLONIUS

My lord, he's going to his mother's room—
Behind the tapestry I'll hide myself,
To hear the meeting—I'll warrant she'll tax him home;
And, as you said, and wisely was it said,
'Tis meet that some more audience than a mother,
Since nature makes them partial, should o'erhear
The speech, from vantage. Fare you well, my liege;
I'll call upon you ere you go to bed,
And tell you what I know.

KING

Thanks, dear my lord.
(*Exit* POLONIUS)

O, my offence is rank, it smells to heaven;
It has the primal eldest curse upon it,
A brother's murder! Pray can I not,
Though inclination be as sharp as will—
My stronger guilt defeats my strong intent. . .
What if this curséd hand
Were thicker than itself with brother's blood,

Is there not rain enough in the sweet heavens
To wash it white as snow? Whereto serves mercy
But to confront the visage of offence?
And what's in prayer but this twofold force,
To be forestalled before we come to fall,
Or pardoned being down? Then I'll look up;
My fault is past. But O, what form of prayer
Can serve my turn? "Forgive me my foul murder"?
That cannot be; since I am still possessed
Of those effects for which I did the murder—
My crown, mine own ambition, and my queen.
May one be pardoned and retain th' offence?
In the corrupted currents of this world
Offence's gilded hand may shove by justice,
And oft 'tis seen the wicked prize itself
Buys out the law; but 'tis not so above;
There is no shuffling, there the action lies
In its true nature, and we ourselves compelled,
Even to the teeth and forehead of our faults,
To give in evidence. What then? what's left?
Try what repentance can; what can it not?
Yet what can it when one can not repent?
O wretched state! O bosom black as death!
O liméd soul, that struggling to be free
Are more engaged! Help, angels! Make attempt!
Bow, stubborn knees; and, heart, with strings of steel,
Be soft as sinews of the new-born babe!
All may be well.

(*Kneels and prays*)

(*Enter* HAMLET. *Impelled by an immediate impulse he whips out his sword and moves to kill the* KING [PASSION]. *Then he stops, his arm arrested in air—how do you kill even a murderer who, defenceless, is kneeling and praying to God?*

[180]

[HONOUR *and* CONSCIENCE.] *He slowly lowers his sword.*
Now he begins to rationalize.)

HAMLET

Now might I do it pat, now he is praying,
And now I'll do't and so he goes to heaven,
And so am I revenged? That would be scrutinized:
A villain kills my father; and for that,
I, his sole son, do this same villain send
To heaven.
Why, this is hire and salary, not revenge.
He took my father grossly, full of bread,
With all his crimes broad blown, as flush as May;
And how his audit stands who knows save heaven?
But in our evidence and course of thought,
'Tis heavy with him; and am I then revenged,
To take him in the purging of his soul,
When he is fit and seasoned for his passage?
No!   (*He sheathes his sword*)
Up, sword, and know you a more horrid moment;
When he is drunk asleep, or in his rage,
Or in th' incestuous pleasure of his bed;
At gaming, swearing, or about some act
That has no relish of salvation in it—
Then trip him, that his heels may kick at heaven,
And that his soul may be as damned and black
As hell, whereto it goes. My mother waits.
This physic but prolongs your sickly days.

(*Exit*)

KING (*Rising*)

My words fly up, my thoughts remain below.
Words without thoughts never to heaven go.

(*Exit*)

[1 8 1]

SCENE 4

THE QUEEN'S BEDROOM—*directly following.*
Enter QUEEN *and* POLONIUS.

POLONIUS

He will come straight. Look you lay home to him;
Tell him his pranks have been too broad to bear with,
And that your grace has screened and stood between
Much heat and him. I'll silence me even here.
Pray you, be blunt with him.

QUEEN

      Fear not for me.
Withdraw, I hear him coming.
  (POLONIUS *hides behind the tapestry.—Enter* HAMLET)

HAMLET *(Curt and dry)*

Now, mother, what's the matter?

QUEEN

Hamlet, you have your father much offended.

HAMLET

Mother, you have my father much offended.

[1 8 2]

QUEEN

Come, come, you answer with a crazy tongue.

HAMLET

Go, go, you question with a wicked tongue.

QUEEN

Why, how now, Hamlet?

HAMLET

What's the matter now?

QUEEN

Have you forgotten who I am?

HAMLET

No, by the cross, not so!
You are the queen, your husband's brother's wife,
And—would it were not so!—you are my mother.

QUEEN

Nay, then, I'll set those to you that can speak.

HAMLET

Come, come, and sit you down; you shall not budge;
You go not till I set you up a glass
Where you may see the inmost part of you.

QUEEN

What will you do? you will not murder me?
Help, help, ho!

POLONIUS (*Behind the tapestry*)

What, ho! help, help, help!

HAMLET (*Drawing his sword*)

How now! a rat! Dead, for a ducat, dead!
(*Makes a pass through the tapestry*)

POLONIUS (*Behind the tapestry*)

O, I am slain! (*Falls and dies*)

QUEEN

O me, what have you done?

HAMLET

Nay, I know not, is it the king?

QUEEN

O, what a rash and bloody deed is this!

HAMLET

A bloody deed—almost as bad, good mother,
As kill a king, and marry with his brother.

QUEEN

As kill a king?

HAMLET

Ay, lady, 'twas my word.
(*Lifts up the tapestry and is shocked to discover* POLO-
NIUS—*dead. Swept by intense anger at himself:*)
You wretched, rash, intruding fool; farewell!
I took you for your master; take your fortune;
You've learned, to be too busy is some danger.
(*Turns to his mother*)

Leave wringing of your hands; peace! sit you down,
And let me wring your heart; for so I shall,
If it be made of penetrable stuff;
If damnéd custom has not brazed it so,
That it be proof and bulwark 'gainst all feeling.

QUEEN

What have I done, that you dare wag your tongue
In noise so rude against me?

HAMLET

Such an act
That blurs the grace and blush of modesty,
Calls virtue hypocrite, takes off the rose
From the fair forehead of an innocent love
And sets a blister there; makes marriage-vows
As false as dicers' oaths, O, such a deed
As from the holy rite of wedding plucks
The very soul, and sweet religion makes
A noise of empty words! Heaven's face does blush,
And this great mass, this solid globe of earth,
With gloom-struck visage, as if doomsday's here,
Is thought-sick at the act.

QUEEN

Ay me, what act,
That roars so loud, and thunders in the index?

HAMLET

(*Holding forth a miniature of his father, and compar-*
ing it with the miniature of CLAUDIUS *which the* QUEEN
is wearing)
Look here, upon this picture, and on this,

[185]

The painted representment of two brothers.
See what a grace was seated on this brow;
Hyperion's curls; the front of Jove himself;
An eye like Mars, to threaten and command;
A posture like the herald Mercury
Just-lighted on a heaven-kissing hill;
A combination and a form indeed,
Where every god did seem to set his seal
To give the world assurance of a man.
This was your husband. Look you now, what follows:
Here is your husband; like a mildewed ear,
Blasting his wholesome brother. Have you eyes?
Could you on this fair mountain leave to feed,
And batten on this moor? Ha! have you eyes?
You cannot call it love, for at your age
The hey-day in the blood is tame, it's humble,
And waits upon the judgement; and what judgement
Would step from this to this? Sense sure you have,
Else could you not have motion, but sure that sense
Is apoplexed; for madness would not err,
Nor sense was e'er by madness so enthralled,
But it reserved some quantity of choice
To serve in such a difference. What devil was it
That thus has cheated you at blindman's buff?
Eyes without feeling, feeling without sight,
Ears without hands or eyes could not so blunder.
O shame! where is thy blush? Rebellious hell,
If you can mutiny in a matron's bones,
To flaming youth let virtue be as wax,
And melt in her own fire. Proclaim no shame
When the compulsive ardour gives the charge,
Since frost itself as actively does burn,
And reason panders will.

QUEEN

O Hamlet, speak no more!
You turn my eyes into my very soul,
And there I see such black and ingrained spots
As will not lose their stain.

HAMLET

Nay, but to live
In the rank sweat of an enseaméd bed,
Stewed in corruption, honeying and making love
Over a nasty sty. . .

QUEEN

Oh, speak to me no more!
These words like daggers enter in my ears.
No more, sweet Hamlet!

HAMLET

A murderer and a villain!
A slave that is not even twentieth part
Of your precedent lord; a clown of a king;
A cutpurse of the empire and the rule,
That from a shelf the precious diadem stole,
And put it in his pocket!

QUEEN

No more!

HAMLET

A king of shreds and patches. . . .

(*Enter* GHOST)

Save me, and hover o'er me with your wings,
You heavenly guards!—What would your gracious figure?

QUEEN

Alas, he's mad!

HAMLET

Do you not come your tardy son to chide,
That, lapsed in time and passion, lets go by
Th' important acting of your dread command?
O, say!

GHOST

Do not forget. This visitation
Is but to whet thy almost blunted purpose.
But look, amazement on thy mother sits;
O, step between her and her fighting soul!
Conceit in weakest bodies strongest works.
Speak to her, Hamlet.

HAMLET

How is it with you, lady?

QUEEN

Alas, how is't with you,
That you do fix your eyes on vacancy,
And with the empty air do hold discourse?
O gentle son,
Upon the heat and flame of your distemper
Sprinkle cool patience. Whereon do you look?

HAMLET

On him, on him! Look you, how pale he glares!
His form and cause conjoined, preaching to stones,
Would make them sensitive.—Do not look upon me,
Lest with this piteous action you convert

My stern intents; then what I have to do
Will want true colour; tears, perchance, for blood.

QUEEN

To whom do you speak this?

HAMLET

Do you see nothing there?

QUEEN

Nothing at all; yet all that is I see.

HAMLET

Nor did you nothing hear?

QUEEN

No, nothing but ourselves.

HAMLET

Why, look you there! look, how it steals away!
My father, in his habit as he lived!
Look, where he goes, even now, out at the portal!

(*Exit* GHOST)

QUEEN

This is the very coinage of your brain!
This bodiless creation madness
Is very cunning in.

HAMLET (*Softly and earnestly*)

"Madness"?
My pulse, as yours, does temperately keep time,
And makes as healthful music. It is not madness

That I have uttered. Mother, for love of grace,
Lay not that flattering unction to your soul,
That not your trespass but my madness speaks;
It will but skin and film the ulcerous place,
While rank corruption, mining all within,
Infects unseen. Confess yourself to heaven;
Repent what's past, avoid what is to come,
And do not spread the compost on the weeds
To make them ranker. Forgive me this my virtue;
For in the fatness of these pursy times
Virtue itself of vice must pardon beg,
Yea, bow and woo for leave to do him good.

QUEEN

O Hamlet, you have cleft my heart in twain.

HAMLET

O, throw away the worser part of it,
And live the purer with the other half.
Good night; but go not to my uncle's bed;
Assume a virtue, if you have it not.
Refrain to-night,
And that shall lend a kind of easiness
To the next abstinence; the next more easy;
For habit oft can change the stamp of nature.
Once more, good night;
When you repent and beg of heaven blessing,
I'll blessing beg of you.—For this same lord,
        (*Pointing to* POLONIUS)
I do repent; but heaven has pleased it so,
To punish me with this and this with me,
That I must be its scourge and minister.
I will remove him, and will answer well

The death I gave him. So, again, good night.
I must be cruel, only to be kind.
Thus bad begins, and worse remains behind.
One word more, good lady.

QUEEN

What shall I do?

HAMLET (*Sternly*)

Not this, by no means, that I bid you do:
Let the bloat king tempt you again to bed,
Pinch wanton on your cheek, call you his mouse,
And let him, for a pair of reechy kisses,
Or paddling in your neck with his damned fingers,
Make you unravel all this matter out,
That I essentially am not in madness,
But mad in craft.

QUEEN

Be you assured, if words be made of breath,
And breath of life, I have no life to breathe
What you have said to me.

HAMLET (*Confides in her*)

I must to England; you know that?

QUEEN

Alas,
I had forgot; it's so concluded on.

HAMLET

There's letters sealed; and my two schoolfellows,
Whom I will trust as I will adders fanged,

They bear the mandate; they must sweep my way,
And marshal me to knavery. Let it work;
For 'tis the sport to have the engineer
Hoist with his own petard; and 't shall go hard
But I will delve one yard below their mines,
And blow them at the moon. O, 'tis most sweet,
When in one line two crafts directly meet.
This man shall set me packing;
I'll lug the corpse into the neighbour room.
Mother, good night. Indeed, this counsellor
Is now most still, most secret, and most grave,
Who was in life a foolish, prating knave.—
Come, sir, to draw toward an end with you.—
Good night, mother.

           (*Exit* HAMLET *dragging out the body of* POLONIUS)

SCENE 5

A ROOM IN THE CASTLE—*directly following.*

Enter KING *and* QUEEN.

QUEEN

Ah, my good lord, what I have seen to-night!

KING

What, Gertrude? How is Hamlet?

QUEEN

Mad as the sea and wind, when both contend
Which is the mightier; in his lawless fit,
Behind the drapery hearing something stir,
Whips out his rapier, cries "A rat, a rat!"
And in this brainsick apprehension kills
The unseen good old man.

KING

O heavy deed!
It had been so with us, had we been there.
His liberty is full of threats to all;
To you yourself, to us, to every one.
Alas, how shall this bloody deed be answered?
It will be laid on us, whose providence
Should have kept short, restrained, and out of touch

This mad young man; but so much was our love,
We would not understand what was most fit,
But, like the owner of a foul disease,
To keep it from divulging, let it feed
Even on the pith of life. Where is he gone?

QUEEN

To draw away the body he has killed;
O'er whom his very madness, like some ore
Among a mineral of metals base,
Shows itself pure—he weeps for what is done.

KING

O Gertrude, come away!
The sun no sooner shall the mountains touch,
But we will ship him hence; and this vile deed
We must, with all our majesty and skill,
Both countenance and excuse. Ho, Guildenstern!
            (*Enter* ROSENCRANTZ *and* GUILDENSTERN)
Friends both, go join you with some further aid;
Hamlet in madness has Polonius slain,
And from his mother's bedroom has he dragged him.
Go seek him out; speak fair, and bring the body.
Into the chapel. I pray you, haste in this.
            (*Exeunt* ROSENCRANTZ *and* GUILDENSTERN)
Come, Gertrude, we'll call up our wisest friends,
And let them know, both what we mean to do,
And what's untimely done. O, come away!
My soul is full of discord and dismay.

                                    (*Exeunt*)

[194]

SCENE 6

ANOTHER ROOM IN THE CASTLE—*directly following.*
Enter HAMLET.

GUILDENSTERN (*O.S.*)

Hamlet!

ROSENCRANTZ (*O.S.*)

Lord Hamlet!
(*Enter* ROSENCRANTZ *and* GUILDENSTERN *with* GUARDS)

ROSENCRANTZ

What have you done, my lord, with the dead body?

HAMLET

Compounded it with dust, whereto it's kin.

ROSENCRANTZ

Tell us where it is, that we may bear it to the chapel.

HAMLET

Do not believe it.

ROSENCRANTZ

Believe what?

HAMLET

That I can keep your secret and not my own. Besides, on being questioned by a sponge, what answer should be made by the son of a king?

ROSENCRANTZ

You take me for a sponge, my lord?

HAMLET

Ay, sir; that soaks up the king's favour, his rewards, his authorities. But such officers do the king best service in the end. He keeps them, like an ape, in the corner of his jaw; first stored, to be last swallowed. When he needs what you have gleaned, it is but squeezing you, and, sponge, you shall be dry again.

ROSENCRANTZ

I understand you not, my lord.

HAMLET

I am glad of it; a knavish speech sleeps in a foolish ear.

ROSENCRANTZ

My lord, you must tell us where the body is, and go with us to the king.

HAMLET

The body is with the king, but the king is not with the body. The king is a thing . . .

GUILDENSTERN

"A thing," my lord?

HAMLET

Of nothing. Take me to him.

(Exeunt)

SCENE 7

Aᴎᴏᴛʜᴇʀ ʀᴏᴏᴍ ɪɴ ᴛʜᴇ ᴄᴀꜱᴛʟᴇ—*directly following.*
Enter ᴋɪɴɢ *and* ᴀᴛᴛᴇɴᴅᴀɴᴛꜱ.

Kɪɴɢ

I have sent to seek him, and to find the body.
How dangerous 'tis to let this man go free!
Yet it won't do to put the law on him;
He's loved by the distracted multitude,
Who like not in their judgement, but their eyes;
And where 'tis so, th' offender's scourge is weighed,
But never the offence. To bear all smooth and even,
This sudden sending him away must seem
Deliberate pause. Diseases desperate grown
By desperate appliance are relieved,
Or not at all.

(Enter ʀᴏꜱᴇɴᴄʀᴀɴᴛᴢ*)*
How now! what has befallen?

Rᴏꜱᴇɴᴄʀᴀɴᴛᴢ

Where the dead body is concealed, my lord,
We cannot get from him.

Kɪɴɢ

But where is he?

Rᴏꜱᴇɴᴄʀᴀɴᴛᴢ

Outside, my lord; guarded, to know your pleasure.

[197]

KING

Bring him before us.

ROSENCRANTZ

Ho, Guildenstern, bring in my lord.

(*Enter* HAMLET, GUILDENSTERN, *and* GUARDS)

KING

Now, Hamlet, where's Polonius?

HAMLET

(*Dropping the least semblance of courtesy due a king*)

At supper.

KING

"At supper"? where?

HAMLET

(*With deliberate rudeness*)

Not where he eats, but where he is eaten. A certain convocation
of politic worms are even now at him. Your worm is your only
emperor for diet. We fat all other creatures to fat us, and we fat
ourselves for maggots. Your fat king and your lean beggar is
but variable service—two dishes, but to one table; that's the end.

KING

Alas, alas! . . . Where is Polonius?

HAMLET

In heaven; send there to see; if your messenger find him not
there, seek him in the other place yourself. But indeed, if you
find him not within this month, you shall nose him as you go up
the stairs into the lobby.

KING (*To some* ATTENDANTS)

Go seek him there.

HAMLET

He will stay till you come.

(*Exeunt* ATTENDANTS)

KING

Hamlet, this deed, for your especial safety—
For which we care as deeply as we grieve
For that which you have done—must send you hence
With fiery quickness. Therefore prepare yourself;
The bark is ready and the wind at help,
The associates wait, and everything is bent
For England.

HAMLET

For England?

KING

Ay, Hamlet.

HAMLET

Good.

KING

So it is, if you knew our purposes.

HAMLET

I see a cherub that sees them. But, come, for England!
    (*Openly mocking the* KING)
Farewell, dear mother.

KING

Your loving father, Hamlet.

HAMLET

My mother. Father and mother is man and wife; man and wife
is one flesh; and so, my mother.—Come, for England!

(*Exit with* GUARDS)

KING

(*To* ROSENCRANTZ *and* GUILDENSTERN *with fury he can
hardly control*)
Follow him at heel, tempt him with speed aboard,
Delay it not, I'll have him hence to-night.
Away! for every thing is sealed and done
That else leans on th' affair; pray you, make haste.

(*Exeunt all but the* KING)

And, England, if my love you hold at aught—
As my great power thereof may give you sense,
Since yet your cicatrice looks raw and red
After the Danish sword, and your free awe
Pays homage to us—you may not coldly set
Our sovereign mandate; which imports in full,
By letters conjuring to that effect,
Th' immediate death of Hamlet. Do it, England;
For like the hectic in my blood he rages,
And you must cure me. Till I know 'tis done,
Whate'er my hopes, my joys have not begun.

(*Exit*)

SCENE 8

A PLAIN IN DENMARK—*shortly following.*
Enter Prince FORTINBRAS, *a* CAPTAIN, *and* SOLDIERS, *marching.*

FORTINBRAS

Go, captain, from me greet the Danish king;
Tell him that by his license Fortinbras
Craves the conveyance of a promised march
Over his kingdom.

CAPTAIN

I will do't, my lord.
(*Exeunt* FORTINBRAS *and* SOLDIERS.
Enter HAMLET, ROSENCRANTZ, GUILDENSTERN, *and others*)

HAMLET

Good sir, whose forces are these?

CAPTAIN

They are of Norway, sir.

HAMLET

How purposed, sir, I pray you?

CAPTAIN

Against some part of Poland.

HAMLET

Who commands them, sir?

CAPTAIN

The nephew to old Norway, Fortinbras.

HAMLET

Goes it against the main of Poland, sir,
Or for some frontier?

CAPTAIN

Truly to speak, and with no exaggeration,
We go to gain a little patch of ground
That has in it no profit but the name.
To pay five ducats, five, I would not rent it;
Nor will it yield to Norway or the Pole
A higher rate, should it be sold in fee.

HAMLET

Why, then the Polack never will defend it.

CAPTAIN

Yes, 'tis already garrisoned.

HAMLET

Two thousand souls and twenty thousand ducats
Will not decide the question of this straw.
This is the cancer of much wealth and peace,
That inward breaks, and shows no cause outside
Why the man dies. I humbly thank you, sir.

CAPTAIN

God be with you, sir.   (*Exit*)

ROSENCRANTZ

Will't please you go, my lord?

HAMLET

I'll be with you straight. Go a little before.

(Exeunt all but HAMLET*)*

How all occasions do inform against me,
And spur my dull revenge! ... What is a man,
If his chief good and purpose of his time
Be but to sleep and feed? a beast, no more.
Sure, He that made us with such power of thought,
Aware of past and future, gave us not
That capability and god-like reason
To mould in us unused. Now, whether it be
Bestial oblivion, or some craven scruple
Of thinking too precisely on the issue—
A thought which, quartered, has but one part wisdom
And ever three parts coward—I do not know
Why yet I live to say "This thing's to do,"
Since I have cause, and will, and strength, and means
To do't. Examples gross as earth exhort me.
Witness this army of such mass and charge,
Led by a delicate and youthful prince,
Whose spirit, with divine ambition puffed,
Makes mouths at the invisible result,
Exposing what is mortal and unsure
To all that fortune, death, and danger dare,
Even for an egg-shell. Rightly to be great
Is not to stir without great argument,
But greatly to find quarrel in a straw
When honour's at the stake. How stand I then,
That have a father killed, a mother stained,
Excitements of my reason and my blood,

And let all sleep, while to my shame I see
The imminent death of twenty thousand men,
That for a fantasy and toy of fame
Go to their graves like beds, fight for a plot
Whereon the numbers cannot try the cause,
Which is not tomb enough and continent
To hide the slain? Oh! from this time forth,
My thoughts be bloody, or be nothing worth!

(Exit)

A C T IV

A C T   IV

S C E N E 1

ELSINORE, A ROOM IN THE CASTLE—*about seven days later.*
Enter QUEEN, HORATIO, *and a* GENTLEMAN.

QUEEN

I will not speak with her.

GENTLEMAN

She is importunate, indeed distracted;
Her mood needs to be pitied.

QUEEN

What would she have?

GENTLEMAN

She speaks much of her father; says she hears
There're tricks in the world, and hems and beats her heart.
Her speech is nothing,
Yet the unshaped use of it does move

The hearers to conclusion—they guess at it,
And botch the words up fit to their own thoughts.

HORATIO

'Twere good she were spoken with; for she may strew
Dangerous conjectures in evil-breeding minds.

QUEEN

Let her come in.

(*Exit* GENTLEMAN)

(*Aside*) To my sick soul, as sin's true nature is,
Each straw seems prologue to some great misfortune.
So full of quick suspicion is one's guilt,
It spills itself in fearing to be spilt.

(*Re-enter* GENTLEMAN, *with* OPHELIA)

OPHELIA

Where is the beauteous majesty of Denmark?

QUEEN

How now, Ophelia!

OPHELIA (*Sings*)

How should I your true love know
From another one?
By his cockle-hat and staff,
And his sandal shoon.

QUEEN

Alas, sweet lady, what imports this song?

OPHELIA

Say you? Nay, pray you, mark.
(*Sings*)   He is dead and gone, lady,

　　　　He is dead and gone;
　　　　At his head a grass-green turf,
　　　　　At his heels a stone.

O, ho!

(Enter KING)

QUEEN

Alas, look here, my lord.

KING

How do you, pretty lady?

OPHELIA

Well, God reward you! They say the owl was a baker's daughter. Lord! we know what we are, but know not what we may be. . . . God be at your table! Pray you, let's have no words of this; but when they ask you what it means, say you this:
(*Sings*)　To-morrow is Saint Valentine's day,
　　　　All in the morning betime,
　　　　And I a maid at your window,
　　　　　To be your Valentine.
　　　　Then up he rose, and donned his clothes,
　　　　　And ope'd the chamber door,
　　　　Let in the maid, that out a maid
　　　　　Never departed more.

KING

Pretty Ophelia!

OPHELIA (*Sings*)

　　By Gis and by Saint Charity,
　　　Alack and fie for shame,
　　Young men will do't if they come to't,
　　　By God, they are to blame.

[209]

> Said she, "Before you tumbled me,
> You promised me to wed."

He answers:

> "So would I ha' done, by yonder sun,
> If you had not come to my bed."

KING

How long has she been thus?

OPHELIA

I hope all will be well. We must be patient; but I cannot choose but weep, to think they should lay him in the cold ground. My brother shall know of it; and so I thank you for your good counsel.—Come, my coach!—Good night, ladies! Good night, sweet ladies! Good night, good night! *(Exit)*

KING

Follow her close; and watch her well, I pray you.

(Exit HORATIO *and* GENTLEMAN*)*

O, this is the poison of deep grief; it springs
All from her father's death. O Gertrude, Gertrude,
When sorrows come, they come not single spies,
But in battalions! First, her father slain;
Next, your son gone, and he most violent author
Of his own just remove; the people muddied,
Thick and unwholesome in their thoughts and whispers
For good Polonius' death—and we were foolish,
In hugger-mugger to inter him—poor Ophelia
Divided from herself and her fair judgement,
Without the which we are but pictures, or mere beasts;
Last, and as important as all these,
Her brother has in secret come from France;
And lacks not gossips to infect his ear

With pestilent speeches of his father's death,
Wherein the slanderers, of matter beggared,
Will stop at nothing to accuse our person
In ear and ear.
  (*A noise O.S.*)

QUEEN

What noise is this?

KING

Where are my Switzers? Let them guard the door.
      (*Enter a* MESSENGER)
What is the matter?

MESSENGER

    Save yourself, my lord!
The ocean, overflowing all his bounds,
Eats not the flats with more impetuous haste
Than young Laertes, with a riotous band,
O'erbears your officers. The rabble call him king;
They cry "Choose we, Laertes shall be king!"
Caps, hands, and tongues applaud it to the clouds,
"Laertes shall be king, Laertes king!"
  (*Noise and shouts O. S.*)

QUEEN

How cheerfully on the false trail they cry!
O, this is treason, you false Danish dogs!
  (*More tumult; sound of breaking doors O. S.*)

KING

The doors are broke.
    (*Enter* LAERTES, *armed;* DANES *following*)

[2 1 1]

LAERTES

Where is this king? Sirs, wait you all outside.

DANES

No, let's come in.

LAERTES

I pray you, give me leave.

DANES

We will, we will.

(*They retire outside the door*)

LAERTES

I thank you. Guard the door.—O you vile king,
Give me my father!

QUEEN

Calmly, good Laertes.

LAERTES

That drop of blood that's calm proclaims me bastard,
Cries cuckold to my father, puts the brand
Of harlot on the chaste unsullied brow
Of my true mother.

(*The* QUEEN *steps in front of* LAERTES, *protecting the*
KING)

KING

What is the cause, Laertes,
That your rebellion looks so giant-like?
Let him go, Gertrude, fear not for our person—
There's such divinity does hedge a king,

That treason can but peep to what it would,
Acts little of his will.—Tell me, Laertes,
Why you are so incensed—Let him go, Gertrude—
Speak, man.

LAERTES

Where is my father?

KING

Dead.

QUEEN

But not by him.

KING

Let him demand his fill.

LAERTES

How came he dead? I'll not be juggled with.
To hell, allegiance! Vows, to the blackest devil!
Conscience and grace, to the profoundest pit!
I dare damnation. To this point I stand:
Let come what comes, only I'll be revenged
Most thoroughly for my father.

KING

Who shall stop you?

LAERTES

My will, not all the world!

KING

Good Laertes,
If you desire to know the certainty
Of your dear father's death, is't writ in your revenge,
That you will swoop upon both friend and foe?

LAERTES

None but his enemies.

KING

> Why, now you speak

Like a good child, and a true gentleman.
That I am guiltless of your father's death,
And am most feelingly in grief for it,
It shall as level to your judgement pierce
As day does to your eye.

DANES (*O.S.*)

> Let her come in.
> (*Re-enter* OPHELIA *with flowers in her hand*)

LAERTES

O heat, dry up my brains! tears seven times salt,
Burn out the sense and power of mine eye!
By heaven, your madness shall be paid with weight,
Till our scale turn the beam. O rose of May!
Dear maid, kind sister, sweet Ophelia!

OPHELIA (*Sings*)

> They bore him barefaced on the bier;
> Hey non nonny, nonny, hey nonny;
> And in his grave rained many a tear ...

Fare you well, my dove!

LAERTES

Had you your wits, and did entreat revenge,
It could not move one thus.

OPHELIA

There's rosemary, that's for remembrance; pray you, love, remember; and there is pansies, that's for thoughts. There's fennel
for you, and columbines. There's rue for you; and here's some
for me; we may call it herb of grace of Sundays. There's a daisy.
I would give you some violets, but they withered all, when my
father died; they say he made a good end . . .
　(*Sings*) For bonny sweet Robin is all my joy . . .

LAERTES

Thought and affliction, passion, hell itself,
She turns to favour and to prettiness.

OPHELIA

　(*Sings*)　And will he not come again?
　　　　　And will he not come again?
　　　　　　No, no, he is dead;
　　　　　　Go to thy death-bed;
　　　　　He never will come again . . .
　　　　　God have mercy on his soul!—
And for all Christian souls, I pray God. God be with you.

(Exit)

LAERTES

Do you see this, O God?

KING

Laertes, I must share with you your grief,
Or else you do me wrong. Go but apart,
Make choice of whom your wisest friends you will,
And they shall hear and judge 'twixt you and me.
If by direct or by collateral hand

They find us touched, we will our kingdom give,
Our crown, our life, and all that we call ours,
To you in satisfaction; but if not,
Be you content to lend your patience to us,
And we shall jointly labour with your soul
To give it due content.

LAERTES

    Let this be so.
His means of death, his obscure funeral—
No noble rite, nor formal ostentation—
Cry to be heard, as 'twere from heaven to earth,
That I must call't in question.

KING

     So you shall;
And where the offence is let the great axe fall.
I pray you, go with me.

         (Exeunt)

SCENE 2

ANOTHER ROOM IN THE CASTLE—*directly following.*
Enter HORATIO *and a* SERVANT.

HORATIO

What are they that would speak with me?

SERVANT

Sea-faring men, sir. They say they have letters for you.

HORATIO

Let them come in.   (*Exit* SERVANT)
(*Aside*) I do not know from what part of the world
I should be greeted, if not from Lord Hamlet.

(*Enter* SAILORS)

FIRST SAILOR

God bless you, sir.

HORATIO

May He bless you too.

FIRST SAILOR

He shall, sir, if it please Him. There's a letter for you sir—it comes from the ambassador that was bound for England—if your name be Horatio, as I am let to know it is.

HORATIO (*Reads*)

"Horatio, when you shall have looked this over, give these fellows some means of access to the king; they have letters for him. Before we were two days old at sea, a pirate of very warlike appointment gave us chase. Finding ourselves too slow of sail, we put on a compelled valour, and in the grapple I boarded them. On the instant they got clear of our ship, so I alone became their prisoner. They have dealt with me like merciful thieves; but they knew what they did: I am to do a good turn for them. Let the king have the letters I have sent, and repair you to me with as much speed as you would fly death. I have words to speak in your ear that will make you dumb, yet they are much too light for the bore of the matter. These good fellows will bring you to where I am. Rosencrantz and Guildenstern hold their course for England—of them I have much to tell you. Farewell. He that you know is yours,

Hamlet."

Come, I will make you way for these your letters;
And do't the speedier, that you may direct me
To him from whom you brought them.

(*Exeunt*)

SCENE 3

ANOTHER ROOM IN THE CASTLE—*directly following.*
Enter KING *and* LAERTES.

KING

Now must your conscience my acquittal seal,
And you must put me in your heart for friend,
Since you have heard, and with a knowing ear,
That he who has your noble father slain
Pursued my life.

LAERTES

It well appears; but tell me
Why did you not proceed against these feats,
So criminal in nature?

KING

Oh, for two special reasons,
Which may to you perhaps seem much unsinewed,
But yet to me they're strong. The queen his mother
Lives almost by his looks; and for myself—
My virtue or my plague, be it whichever of the two—
She's so conjunctive to my life and soul,
That, as the star moves not but in his sphere,
I could not but by her. The other motive,
Why to a public count I might not go,

Is the great love the common people bear him;
Who, dipping all his faults in their affection,
Would, like the spring that changes wood to stone,
Convert his shackles to graces; so that my arrows,
Too slightly timbered for so loud a wind,
Would have reverted to my bow again,
And not where I had aimed them.

LAERTES

And so have I a noble father lost;
A sister driven into desperate terms.
But my revenge will come.

KING

Break not your sleep for that; you must not think
That we are made of stuff so flat and dull
That we can let our beard be shook with danger
And think it pastime. You shortly shall hear more.
I loved your father, and I love myself,
And that, I hope, will teach you to imagine . . .
                    (*Enter a* MESSENGER *with two letters*)
How now! what news?

MESSENGER

                    Letters, my lord, from Hamlet.
This to your majesty; this to the queen.
        (*Hands both letters to the* KING)

KING

From Hamlet? Who brought them?

MESSENGER

Sailors, my lord, they say; I saw them not,
They were given me by Claudio; he received them.

KING

Laertes, you shall hear them.
Leave us.   (*Exit* MESSENGER)
(*Reads*) "High and Mighty,—You shall know I am set naked
on your kingdom. Tomorrow shall I beg leave to see your kingly
eyes; when I shall, first asking your permission, recount the
occasion of my sudden and most strange return.

                                             Hamlet."
What can this mean? Have all the rest come back?
Or is it some deception?

LAERTES

                         Know you the hand?

KING

'Tis Hamlet's writing. "Naked!"
And in a postscript here he says, "alone."
        (*Hurriedly opens the* QUEEN's *letter—finding no added
        information there, irritably puts it away. Unnerved*:)
Can you advise me?

LAERTES

I'm lost in it, my lord. But let him come!
It warms the very sickness in my heart,
That I shall live to tell him to his teeth:
"Thus, you now die."

KING

                    If it be so, Laertes,
Will you be ruled by me?

LAERTES

                        Ay, my lord,
So long as you don't rule me to a peace.

KING

To your own peace. If he has now returned,
Thus shying from his voyage, and that he means
No more to undertake it, I will work him
To an exploit now ripe in my device,
Under the which he shall not choose but fall;
And for his death no breath of blame shall touch us,
But even his mother shall acquit the plot
And call it accident.

LAERTES

My lord, I will be ruled;
The more, if you could devise it so
That I might be the organ.

KING

It falls right.
You have been talked of since your travel much,
And that in Hamlet's hearing, for a quality
Wherein, they say, you shine. And all your gifts
Did not together pluck such envy from him,
As did that one.

LAERTES

What gift is that, my lord?

KING

A very ribbon in the cap of youth.
Two months since,
Here was a gentleman of Normandy,
Who gave you such a masterly report
For art and exercise in your defence,
And for your rapier most especially,

That he cried out, 'twould be a sight indeed
If one could match you. The fencers of their nation,
He swore, had neither motion, guard, nor eye,
If you opposed them. Sir, this report of his
Did Hamlet so envenom with his envy
That he could nothing do but wish and beg
Your sudden coming o'er to fence with him.
Now, out of this . . .

LAERTES

What out of this, my lord?

KING

Laertes, was your father dear to you?
Or are you like the painting of a sorrow,
A face without a heart?

LAERTES

Why ask you this?

KING

Not that I think you did not love your father;
But that I know love is subdued by time,
And that I see, in instances of proof,
Time qualifies the spark and fire of it.
There lives within the very flame of love
A kind of wick or snuff that will abate it;
And nothing is of a like goodness always,
For goodness, growing to repletion,
Dies of its own excess. That we would do
We should do when we would; for this "would" changes,
And has abatements and delays as many
As there are tongues, are hands, are accidents.

But, to the quick o' the ulcer:
Hamlet comes back; what would you undertake
To show yourself your father's son in deed
More than in words?

LAERTES

To cut his throat in the church.

KING

No place indeed should murder sanctuarize;
Revenge should have no bounds. But, good Laertes,
Will you do this, keep close within your chamber.
Hamlet returned shall know you have come home.
We'll get some friends to praise your excellence
And set a double varnish on the fame
The Frenchman gave you; bring you then together,
And wager on your heads. He, being careless,
Most generous, and free from all contriving,
Will not peruse the foils; so that with ease,
Or with a little shuffling, you may choose
The one unblunted sword, and in a pass of practice
Requite him for your father.

LAERTES

I will do it.
And for that purpose I'll anoint my sword.
I bought an ointment of a mountebank,
So mortal, that but dip a knife in it,
Where it draws blood, no cataplasm so rare
Can save the thing from death. I'll touch my point
With this contagion, that, if I gall him slightly,
It may be death.

KING

I further think this project
Should have a back or second, that might hold
If this should blast in proof. Soft! let me see . . .
We'll make a solemn wager on your skills . . .
I have it:
When in your motion you are hot and dry—
You make your bouts more violent to that end—
And when he calls for drink, I'll have prepared him
A chalice for that moment, which but sipping,
If he by chance escape your venomed thrust,
Our purpose may hold there. But wait, what noise?

(*Enter* QUEEN)

How now, sweet queen?

QUEEN

One woe does tread upon another's heel,
So fast they follow. Your sister's drowned, Laertes.

LAERTES

Drowned! O, where?

QUEEN

There is a willow grows aslant a brook,
That shows his gray leaves in the glassy stream.
There with fantastic garlands did she come
Of crow-flowers, nettles, daisies, and long purples;
There, on the pendent boughs her coronet weeds
Clambering to hang, an envious branch broke off,
When down her weedy trophies and herself
Fell in the weeping brook. Her clothes spread wide,
And, mermaid-like, awhile they bore her up;

[225]

Which time she chanted snatches of old tunes;
Till that her garments, heavy with their drink,
Pulled the poor dear from her melodious lay
To muddy death.

LAERTES

Alas, then she is drowned?

QUEEN

Drowned, drowned.

LAERTES

My lord,
I have a speech of fire, that fain would blaze,
But that my tears do drown it.   (*Exit*)

KING

Let's follow, Gertrude.
How much I had to do to calm his rage!
Now fear I this will give it start again.

(*Exeunt*)

SCENE 4

A CHURCHYARD—*next day.*
Enter two GRAVEDIGGERS, *with spades, etc. They begin to prepare a grave.*

FIRST GRAVEDIGGER

Is she to be buried in Christian burial, who wilfully seeks her own damnation?

SECOND GRAVEDIGGER

I tell you she is; the coroner has sat on her, and finds it Christian burial.

FIRST GRAVEDIGGER

How can that be, unless she drowned herself in her own defence?

SECOND GRAVEDIGGER

Why, 'tis found so.

FIRST GRAVEDIGGER

It must be "se offendendo"; it cannot be else. For here lies the point: if I drown myself wittingly, it argues an act; and an act has three branches: it is to act, to do, and to perform—argal, she drowned herself wittingly.

SECOND GRAVEDIGGER

Nay, but hear you, goodman digger, . . .

FIRST GRAVEDIGGER

Give me leave. Here lies the water—good. Here stands the man—good. If the man go to this water and drown himself, it is, will he nill he, he goes—mark you that. But if the water come to him and drown him, he drowns not himself. Argal, he that is not guilty of his own death shortens not his own life.

SECOND GRAVEDIGGER

But is this law?

FIRST GRAVEDIGGER

Ay, marry, it is; coroner's quest law.

SECOND GRAVEDIGGER

Will you have the truth of it? If this had not been a gentle-woman, she should have been buried out of Christian burial.

FIRST GRAVEDIGGER

Why, you said it!—Come, my spade! There is no ancient gentle-men but gardeners, ditchers, and grave-makers; they hold up Adam's profession.

SECOND GRAVEDIGGER

Was he a gentleman?

FIRST GRAVEDIGGER

He was the first that ever bore arms.

SECOND GRAVEDIGGER

Why, he had none.

FIRST GRAVEDIGGER

What, are you a heathen? How do you understand the Scripture? The Scripture says "Adam digged"; could he dig without arms? I'll put another question to you. If you answer me not to the purpose, confess yourself . . .

SECOND GRAVEDIGGER

Go to.

FIRST GRAVEDIGGER

Who is he that builds stronger than either the mason, the shipwright, or the carpenter?

SECOND GRAVEDIGGER

The gallows-maker; for that frame outlives a thousand tenants.

FIRST GRAVEDIGGER

I like your wit well, in good faith; the gallows does well. But how does it well? It does well to those that do ill. Now you do ill to say the gallows is built stronger than the church; argal, the gallows may do well to you. To it again; come.

SECOND GRAVEDIGGER

"Who builds stronger than a mason, a shipwright, or a carpenter?"

FIRST GRAVEDIGGER

Ay, tell me that.

SECOND GRAVEDIGGER

Marry, now I can tell.

FIRST GRAVEDIGGER

To it.

SECOND GRAVEDIGGER

By the Mass, I cannot tell.

(*Enter* HAMLET *and* HORATIO, *afar off*)

FIRST GRAVEDIGGER

Cudgel your brains no more about it, for your dull ass will not mend his pace with beating; and, when you are asked this question next, say "a grave-maker." The houses that he makes last till doomsday. Go, get you to Yaughan, and fetch me a tankard of liquor.

(*Exit* SECOND GRAVEDIGGER)

(*He digs, and sings*)

> In youth, when I did love, did love,
> Methought it was very sweet,
> To contract, O, the time for-a my behove,
> O, methought, there was nothing meet.

HAMLET

Has this fellow no feeling of his business, that he sings at grave-making?

HORATIO

Custom has made him easy in it.

FIRST GRAVEDIGGER (*Sings*)

> But age with his stealing steps
> Hath clawed me in his clutch,
> And hath shipped me into the land,
> As if I had never been such.

(*Throws up a skull*)

HAMLET

That skull had a tongue in it, and could sing once! How the knave dashes it to the ground, as if it were Cain's jaw-bone, him that did the first murder! It might be the pate of a politician, one who would circumvent God, whom this ass now gets the better of; might it not?

HORATIO

It might, my lord.

HAMLET

Or of a courtier; who could say, "Good-morrow, sweet lord! How do you, good lord?"

HORATIO

Ay, my lord.
(FIRST GRAVEDIGGER *throws up another skull*)

HAMLET

There's another. Why may not that be the skull of a lawyer? Where are his legal subtleties now, his quibbles, his cases, his tenures, and his tricks? Why does he suffer this rude knave now to knock him about the sconce with a dirty shovel, and will not tell him of his action of battery? I will speak to this fellow.— Whose grave's this, sirrah?

FIRST GRAVEDIGGER

Mine, sir.
(*Sings*)   O, a pit of clay for to be made
For such a guest is meet.

HAMLET

I think it is yours, indeed, for you lie in it.

FIRST GRAVEDIGGER

You lie out of it, sir, and therefore 'tis not yours. For my part, I do not lie in it, and yet it is mine.

[2 3 1]

HAMLET

You do lie in it, to be in it and say it is yours. 'Tis for the dead, not for the quick; therefore you lie.

FIRST GRAVEDIGGER

'Tis a quick lie, sir; 'twill away again, from me to you.

HAMLET

What man do you dig it for?

FIRST GRAVEDIGGER

For no man, sir.

HAMLET

What woman, then?

FIRST GRAVEDIGGER

For none, neither.

HAMLET

Who is to be buried in it?

FIRST GRAVEDIGGER

One that was a woman, sir; but, rest her soul, she's dead.

HAMLET (*To* HORATIO)

How absolute the knave is! we must speak precisely to the point, or equivocation will undo us. By the Lord, Horatio, this three years I have taken note of it, the age is grown so affected, that the peasant sophisticates almost as glibly as the courtier.—How long have you been a grave-maker?

FIRST GRAVEDIGGER

Of all the days in the year, I came to it that day that our last king
Hamlet overcame Fortinbras.

HAMLET

How long is that since?

FIRST GRAVEDIGGER

Cannot you tell that? every fool can tell that. It was the very day
that young Hamlet was born; he that is mad, and sent into
England.

HAMLET

Ay, marry, why was he sent into England?

FIRST GRAVEDIGGER

Why, because he was mad. He shall recover his wits there; or,
if he do not, it's no great matter there.

HAMLET

Why?

FIRST GRAVEDIGGER

'Twill not be seen in him there; there the men are as mad as he.

HAMLET

How came he mad?

FIRST GRAVEDIGGER

Very strangely, they say.

HAMLET

How "strangely"?

FIRST GRAVEDIGGER

Faith, even with losing his wits.

HAMLET

Upon what ground?

FIRST GRAVEDIGGER

Why, here in Denmark. I have been sexton here, man and boy, twenty years.

HAMLET

How long will a man lie in the earth ere he rot?

FIRST GRAVEDIGGER

Faith, if he be not rotten before he die—as we have many pocky corpses now-a-days that will scarce hold till the laying in—he will last you some eight year, or nine year. A tanner will last you nine year.

HAMLET

Why he more than another?

FIRST GRAVEDIGGER

Why, sir, his hide is so tanned with his trade, that he will keep out water a great while; and your water is a sore decayer of your whoreson dead body. Here's a skull now; this skull has lain in the earth thirteen years.

HAMLET

Whose was it?

FIRST GRAVEDIGGER

A whoreson mad fellow's it was; whose do you think it was?

HAMLET

Nay, I know not.

FIRST GRAVEDIGGER

A pestilence on him, the mad rogue! He poured a flagon of Rhenish wine on my head once. This same skull, sir, was Yorick's skull, the king's jester.

HAMLET

This?

FIRST GRAVEDIGGER

Even that.

HAMLET

Let me see. (*Takes the skull*) Alas, poor Yorick! I knew him, Horatio. A fellow of infinite jest, of most excellent fancy. He has borne me on his back a thousand times. And now how abhorred in my imagination it is! my gorge rises at it: here hung those lips that I have kissed I know not how often.—Where are your gibes now? your gambols, your songs, your flashes of merriment, that used to set the table in a roar? Not one now, to mock your own grinning? quite grim? Now go you to a lady's dressing room, and tell her, let her paint her face an inch thick, to this aspect she must come. Make her laugh at that.—Pray you, Horatio, tell me one thing.

HORATIO

What's that, my lord?

HAMLET

Do you think Alexander looked in this fashion in the earth?

HORATIO

Even so.

HAMLET

And smelt so? pah! (*Puts down the skull*)

HORATIO

Even so, my lord.

HAMLET

To what base uses we may return, Horatio! Why may not imagination trace the noble dust of Alexander till it find it stopping
a bung-hole?

HORATIO

It's to consider too curiously, to consider so.

HAMLET

No, faith, not a jot: Alexander died, Alexander was buried,
Alexander returned into dust; the dust is earth, of earth we make
loam, and why with that loam, whereto he was converted, might
they not stop a beer-barrel?
   Imperious Caesar, dead and turned to clay,
   Might stop a hole to keep the wind away.
   O, that that earth, which kept the world in awe,
   Should patch a wall to expel the winter's flaw!
But soft! but soft! aside! here comes the king.
         (*Enter a funeral procession: the corpse of* OPHELIA *in
         an open coffin*, LAERTES, KING, QUEEN, *their trains*,
         PRIEST, *etc.*)
The queen, the courtiers; who is that they follow?

And with such maiméd rites? This does betoken,
The corpse they follow did with desperate hand
Destroy its own life. 'Twas of some estate.
Let us retreat awhile, and mark.
    (*Retiring with* HORATIO)

LAERTES

What other ceremony?

HAMLET

                        That is Laertes,
A very noble youth. Mark.

LAERTES

What other ceremony?

PRIEST

Her obsequies have been as far enlarged
As we have warranty; her death was doubtful;
And, but that great command o'ersways the rule,
She should in ground unsanctified have lodged
Till the last trumpet.

LAERTES

Must there no more be done?

PRIEST

                        "No more be done?"
We should profane the service of the dead
To sing a requiem and such rest to her
As to in peace departed souls.

LAERTES

Lay her in the earth,
And from her fair and unpolluted flesh
May violets spring!
(*The coffin is being lowered into the grave*)
I tell you, churlish priest,
A ministering angel shall my sister be,
When you in hell are howling.

HAMLET

What? the fair Ophelia?

QUEEN (*Scattering flowers*)

Sweets to the sweet! Farewell!
I hoped you should have been my Hamlet's wife;
I thought your bride-bed to have decked, sweet maid,
And not have strewn your grave.

LAERTES

O, treble woe
Fall ten times treble on that curséd head,
Whose wicked deed your most ingenious sense
Deprived you of!—Hold off the earth awhile,
Till I have caught her once more in my arms.
(*Leaps into the grave*)
Now pile your dust upon the quick and dead,
Till of this flat a mountain you have made
To o'ertop old Pelion, or the sky-high head
Of blue Olympus.

HAMLET (*Advancing*)

What is he whose grief
Bears such an emphasis? whose phrase of sorrow

[238]

Conjures the wandering stars, and makes them stand
Like wonder-wounded hearers? This is I,
Hamlet the Dane.

LAERTES

The devil take your soul!
(*Leaps out of the grave and grapples* HAMLET)

HAMLET (*With deadly calm*)

You pray not well.
I pray you, take your fingers from my throat,
For, though I'm not irascible and rash,
Yet have I in me something dangerous,
Which let your wisdom fear. Hold off your hand.
(*This has no effect on* LAERTES. *They scuffle*)

KING

Pluck them asunder.

QUEEN

Hamlet, Hamlet!

ALL

Gentlemen! . . .

HORATIO

Good my lord, be quiet.
(HORATIO *and the* ATTENDANTS *part them*)

HAMLET

Why, I will fight with him upon this theme
Until my eyelids will no longer wag.

[239]

QUEEN

O my son, what theme?

HAMLET

I loved Ophelia. Forty thousand brothers
Could not, with all their quantity of love,
Make up my sum.—What will you do for her?

KING

O, he is mad, Laertes.

QUEEN

For love of God, forbear him.

HAMLET

'Swounds, show me what you'll do;
Will weep? will fight? will fast? will tear yourself?
Will drink up eisel? eat a crocodile?
I'll do't. Do you come here to whine?
To outface me with leaping in her grave?
Be buried quick with her, and so will I.
And, if you prate of mountains, let them throw
Millions of acres on us, till our ground,
Singeing its pate against the burning zone,
Make Ossa like a wart! Nay, if you'll mouth,
I'll rant as well as you.

QUEEN

              This is mere madness;
And thus awhile the fit will work on him;
Anon, as patient as the female dove,
Before her golden chicks are hatched,
His silence will sit drooping.

HAMLET

Hear you, sir,
What is the reason that you use me thus?
I loved you ever. But it is no matter;
Let Hercules himself do what he may,
The cat will mew, and dog will have his day.

(Exit)

KING

I pray you, good Horatio, wait upon him.

(Exit HORATIO)

(Aside to LAERTES)
Strengthen your patience with our last night's speech;
We'll put the matter to the instant test.—
Good Gertrude, set some watch over your son.—
This grave shall have a living monument.

(Exeunt)

SCENE 5

A HALL IN THE CASTLE—*shortly following.*
        Enter HAMLET *and* HORATIO.

HAMLET

So much for this; now shall you see the other.
You do remember all the circumstances?

HORATIO

Remember it, my lord!

HAMLET

Sir, in my heart there was a kind of fighting,
That would not let me sleep. So, rashly—
And praised be rashness, for it lets us know,
Our indiscretion sometimes serves us well
When our deep plots do fail; and that should teach us
There's a divinity that shapes our ends,
Rough-hew them how we will—

HORATIO

        That is most certain.

HAMLET

Up from my cabin,
My sea-gown thrown about me, in the dark

I groped to find them out; had my desire,
Fingered their packet, and in short withdrew
To my own room again; making so bold,
My fears forgetting manners, to unseal
Their grand commission; where I found, Horatio—
O royal knavery!—an exact command,
Tricked out with many several sorts of reasons,
That, on the reading, not a minute lost,
My head should be struck off.

HORATIO

Is't possible?

HAMLET (*Giving him the scroll*)

Here's the commission; read it at more leisure.
Being thus be-netted round with villainies,
Ere I could make a prologue to my brains,
They had begun the play. I sat me down;
Devised a new commission; wrote it neatly:
An earnest conjuration from the king,
As England was his faithful tributary,
That, right upon the learning of these contents,
He should the bearers put to sudden death,
And no confession-time allowed.

HORATIO

How was this sealed?

HAMLET

Why, even in that was heaven provident.
I had my father's signet in my purse.
Which was the model of that Danish seal;
Folded the writ up in the form of the other;

[243]

Subscribed it; gave't the impression; placed it safely,
The changeling never known. Now, the next day
Was our sea-fight; and what to this was sequent
You know already.

HORATIO

So Guildenstern and Rosencrantz go to their death.

HAMLET

Why, man, they did make love to this employment;
They are not near my conscience; their destruction
Is by their own insinuation brought.
It's dangerous when the smaller people come
Between the sword-points and the deadly thrusts
Of mighty opposites.

HORATIO

                Why, what a king is this!

HAMLET

Does it not, think you, fall upon me now—
He that has killed my king, and whored my mother;
Popped in between th' election and my hopes;
Thrown out his hook and line for my own life,
And with such trickery—is't not perfect conscience
To quit him with this arm? And is't not to be damned,
To let this cancer of our nature come
To further evil?

HORATIO

It must be shortly known to him from England
What is the issue of the business there.

HAMLET

It will be short; the interim is mine;
And a man's life's no more than to say "One."
But I am very sorry, good Horatio,
That to Laertes I forgot myself;
For by the image of my cause I see
The portraiture of his. I'll court his favours.
But sure the bombast of his grief did put me
Into a towering passion.

HORATIO

                  Peace! who comes here?
(*Enter young* OSRIC, *new at the Court. He is trying to achieve the height of courtliness in his deportment, and is overdoing it*)

OSRIC

(*Taking off his fashionable hat, and with an elaborate bow*)
Your lordship is right welcome back to Denmark.

HAMLET

I humbly thank you, sir. (*Aside to* HORATIO) Do you know this water-fly?

HORATIO (*Aside to* HAMLET)

No, my good lord.

HAMLET (*Aside to* HORATIO)

Your state is the more gracious. He has much land, and fertile.
Let a beast be lord of beasts, and he shall eat at the king's table.
He's a boor; but, as I say, rich in the possession of dirt.

OSRIC

(*With another bow, making sweeping gestures with his hat*)

Sweet lord, if your lordship were at leisure, I should impart a thing to you from his majesty.

HAMLET

I will receive it, sir, with all diligence of spirit.
Put your bonnet to its right use, 'tis for the head.

OSRIC

I thank your lordship, it is very hot.

HAMLET

No, believe me, 'tis very cold; the wind is northerly.

OSRIC

It is somewhat cold, my lord, indeed.

HAMLET

But yet, I think, it is very sultry and hot, for my temperament.

OSRIC

Exceedingly, my lord; it is very sultry, as 'twere—I cannot tell how.... But, my lord, his majesty bade me signify to you that he has laid a great wager on your head. Sir, this is the matter....

HAMLET

I beseech you, remember....

(HAMLET *gestures him to put on his hat*)

OSRIC

Nay, good my lord, for mine ease, in good faith. Sir, here is newly come to court Laertes; believe me, an absolute gentleman, full of most distinctive excellences, of very refined manners and noble appearance; indeed, to speak feelingly of him, he is the very guide-book of gentility; for you shall find him to be the container of all the qualities a gentleman would expect.

HAMLET

Sir, his definement suffers no perdition in you, though I know, to divide him inventorially would dizzy the arithmetic of memory. But, in the verity of extolment, I take him to be a soul of great article. The concernancy, sir? why do we wrap the gentleman in our more rawer breath?

OSRIC

Sir?

HAMLET

What imports the nomination of this gentleman?

OSRIC

Of Laertes?

HORATIO (*Aside to* HAMLET)

His purse is empty already, all his golden words are spent.

HAMLET

Of him, sir.

OSRIC

I know you are not ignorant of what excellence Laertes is. . . .

HAMLET

I dare not say I know him, lest I should pretend to be his equal in excellence; for, no man can know another well, but by knowing himself.

OSRIC

I mean, sir, for the skill with which he uses his weapon.
His reputation is that in his merit he has no equal.

HAMLET

What's his weapon?

OSRIC

Rapier and dagger.

HAMLET

That's two of his weapons; but, go on.

OSRIC

The king, sir, has wagered with him six Barbary horses; against
the which he has imponed, as I take it, six French rapiers and
poniards, with their assigns, as girdle, hangers, and so. Three of
the carriages, in faith, are very dear to fancy, very responsive to
the hilts, most delicate carriages, and of very liberal conceit.

HAMLET

What call you the carriages?

OSRIC

The carriages, sir, are the hangers.

HAMLET

The phrase would be more germane to the matter, if we could
carry a cannon by our sides; I would it might be hangers till then.
But, on! six Barbary horses against six French swords, their assigns, and three liberal-conceited carriages; that's the French bet
against the Danish. Why is this "imponed," as you call it?

OSRIC

The king, sir, has laid, sir, that in a dozen passes between yourself
and Laertes, he shall not exceed you three hits; and it would
come to immediate trial, if your lordship would vouchsafe the
answer.

HAMLET

How if I answer "No"?

OSRIC

I mean, my lord, the opposition of your person in trial.

HAMLET

Sir, I will walk here in the hall. If it please his majesty, it is the
breathing time of day with me. Let the foils be brought, the
gentleman willing, and the king hold his purpose, I will win for
him if I can; if not, I will gain nothing but my shame and the odd
hits.

OSRIC

Shall I re-deliver you even so?

HAMLET

To this effect, sir, after what flourish your nature will.

OSRIC

I commend my duty to your lordship.

HAMLET

Yours, yours.   (*Exit* OSRIC, *finally putting on his hat*)

HORATIO

This lapwing runs away with the shell on his head.

HAMLET

He must have observed ceremonial courtesy with his mother's nipple before he sucked it. Thus has he—and many more of the same breed that I know the drossy age dotes on—only got the tune of the time and the outward manners of politeness, a kind of frothy talk, which carries them through and through the most foolish and refined opinions; and yet if you just blow to test them—the bubbles are out.

(Enter a LORD*)*

LORD

My lord, his majesty commended himself to you by young Osric, who brings back to him, that you await him in the hall. He sends to know if your pleasure holds to play with Laertes, or that you will take longer time.

HAMLET

I am constant to my purposes; they follow the king's pleasure. If his fitness speaks, mine is ready; now or whensoever, provided I be so able as now.

LORD

The king, and queen, and all are coming down.

HAMLET

In happy time.

LORD

The queen desires you to use some gentle courtesy to Laertes before you fall to play.

HAMLET

She well instructs me.

(Exit LORD*)*

[2 5 0]

HORATIO

You will lose this wager, my lord.

HAMLET

I do not think so. Since he went into France, I have been in continual practice; I shall win at the odds. But you would not know how ill all's here about my heart. But it is no matter.

HORATIO

Nay, good my lord . . .

HAMLET

It is but foolery; but it is such a kind of misgiving as would perhaps trouble a woman.

HORATIO

If your mind dislike any thing, obey it. I will forestall their coming here, and say you are not fit.

HAMLET

Not a whit; we defy augury. There is a special providence in the fall of a sparrow. If it be now, 'tis not to come; if it be not to come, it will be now; if it be not now, yet it will come; the readiness is all. Since no man knows aught of what life has in store for him, what is it to leave betimes? Let be.
(*Enter* KING, QUEEN, LAERTES, *and all the Court;* OSRIC, *carrying foils,* ATTENDANTS *with a table, flagons of wine, cups, etc.*)

KING

Come, Hamlet, come and take this hand from me.
(*The* KING *puts* LAERTES' *hand into* HAMLET'S)

[2 5 1]

HAMLET

Give me your pardon, sir. I've done you wrong;
But pardon't, as you are a gentleman.
This noble gathering knows,
And you must needs have heard, how I am punished
With sore distraction. What I have done,
That might your nature, honour, and objection
Roughly awake, I here proclaim was madness.
Sir, in this audience,
Let my disclaiming from a purposed evil
Free me so far in your most generous thoughts,
That I have shot my arrow o'er the house
And hurt my brother.

LAERTES

I'm satisfied in my own personal feeling,
Whose motive in this case should stir me most
To my revenge; but in my terms of honour
I stand aloof, and will no reconcilement,
Till by some experts in the code of honour
I have a voice and precedent of peace,
To keep my name ungored. But till that time,
I do receive your offered love like love,
And will not wrong it.

HAMLET

           I embrace it freely,
And will this brother's wager frankly play.—
Give us the foils. Come on.

LAERTES

             Come, one for me.
(*The* KING *moves toward the table upon which* OSRIC *is
now placing six or seven foils*)

HAMLET

I'll be your foil, Laertes; in my ignorance
Your skill shall, like a star in the darkest night,
Shine brilliantly indeed.

LAERTES

                              You mock me, sir.

HAMLET

No, by this hand.

KING

    (*By now he has reached the table, spotted the one sharp
sword, and placed himself in such a position that* OSRIC
can pick up only blunt foils)
Give them the foils, young Osric.
    (OSRIC *takes two foils, and moves toward* LAERTES *and*
HAMLET. *The* KING *goes with him*)
                              Nephew Hamlet,
You know the wager?

HAMLET

                              Very well, my lord;
Your grace has laid the bet on the weaker side.

KING

I do not fear it; I have seen you both;
But since you are bettered, we have therefore odds.
    (OSRIC *offers the foils, first to* HAMLET, *then to*
LAERTES)

LAERTES

This is too heavy; let me see another.
    (*Goes to the table, puts his foil down, and from the*

[253]

several others picks the one unblunted and poisoned foil)

HAMLET

I like this well.—These foils have all a length?

OSRIC

Ay, my good lord.

(They prepare to play)

KING

Set me the cups of wine upon the table.
If Hamlet give the first or second hit,
Or quit in answer of the third exchange,
Let all the battlements their cannon fire.
The king shall drink to Hamlet's better breath;
And he shall throw into the cup a pearl,
Richer than that which four successive kings
In Denmark's crown have worn. Give me the cups;
And let the kettle-drum to the trumpet speak,
The trumpet to the cannoneer without,
The cannons to the heavens, the heavens to earth,
"Now the king drinks to Hamlet."—Come, begin.
And you, the judges, bear a wary eye.

HAMLET

Come on, sir.

LAERTES

Come, my lord.   *(They play)*

HAMLET

One.

LAERTES

No.

HAMLET

Judgement.

OSRIC

A hit, a very palpable hit.

LAERTES

Well; again.

KING

Wait; give me drink.
(ATTENDANT *fills a cup, and gives it to the* KING. *The* KING *holds in his left hand what seems to be a pearl*)
Hamlet, this pearl is yours;
Here's to your health!
(*Drinks a sip or two. The kettle-drums and trumpets sound, and cannon shot O.S. The* KING *drops the "pearl" into the cup, and hands it to the* ATTENDANT)
Give him the cup.

HAMLET

I'll play this bout first; set it by awhile.
(ATTENDANT *puts the cup on a table near by*)
Come. (*They play*) Another hit; what say you?

LAERTES

A touch, a touch, I do confess.

KING

Our son shall win.

[255]

QUEEN

                    He's hot, and scant of breath—
Here, Hamlet, take my kerchief, rub your brow.
            (*Takes the cup from the table*)
The queen is drinking to your fortune, Hamlet.

HAMLET

Good madam!

KING

                    Gertrude, do not drink.

QUEEN

I will, my lord, I pray you, pardon me.
            (*Drinks a few sips*)

KING (*Aside*)

It is the poisoned cup! it is too late!
            (*Now the* QUEEN *offers the cup to* HAMLET)

HAMLET

I dare not drink yet, madam; by and by.

QUEEN

Come, let me wipe your face.   (*Does so*)

LAERTES (*To the* KING)

My lord, I'll hit him now.

KING

                    I do not think so.

LAERTES (*Aside*)

And yet it is almost against my conscience.

HAMLET

Come, for the third, Laertes; you but dally;
I pray you, pass with your best violence;
I am afraid you make a wanton of me.

LAERTES

Say you so? come on.   (*They play*)

OSRIC

Nothing, either way.
> (*They break off. The* KING *glares at* LAERTES *with
> anger.* LAERTES *suddenly assaults* HAMLET, *who is off
> his guard*)

LAERTES

Have at you now!
> (LAERTES *wounds* HAMLET *in the arm.* HAMLET, *enraged
> by this treachery, attacks* LAERTES *with the prime pur-
> pose of knocking the sharp sword out of his hand. He
> does so, picks it up, and throws his own blunt weapon
> to* LAERTES. *They close in again—*HAMLET *fighting with
> cold fury*)

KING

Part them! they are incensed.

HAMLET

Nay, come, again.   (*The* QUEEN *falls*)

[257]

Osric

      Look to the queen there, ho!
*(*HAMLET *wounds* LAERTES *deeply)*

Horatio

They bleed on both sides!—How is it, my lord?

Osric

How is it, Laertes?

Laertes

Why, as a woodcock to my own trap, Osric!
I am justly killed with my own treachery.

Hamlet

How does the queen?

King

      She swoons to see them bleed.

Queen

No, no, the drink, the drink—O my dear Hamlet!
   (*The* KING *slowly begins to make his way through the
   courtiers to leave the hall)*
The drink, the drink! I am poisoned!   (*Dies*)

Hamlet

   (*Seeing the* KING's *chair unoccupied, searches for him
   with his eyes)*
O villainy! Ho! let the door be locked!
Treachery! Seek it out!
   (*Spots the* KING, *and, with a leap, bars his way)*

LAERTES

It is here, Hamlet. Hamlet, you are slain;
No medicine in the world can do you good;
In you there is not half an hour of life;
The treacherous instrument is in your hand,
Unbated and envenomed. The foul plot
Has turned itself on me; so, here I lie,
Never to rise again. Your mother's poisoned.
I can no more—the king—the king's to blame.

HAMLET

The point envenomed too!
Then, venom, do your work.   (*Stabs the* KING)

ALL

Treason! treason! ...

KING

O, yet defend me, friends; I am but hurt.

HAMLET

    (*Seizes the poisoned cup, and forces the contents into
    the* KING's *mouth*)
Here, you incestuous, murderous, damnéd Dane,
Drink off this potion! Is your "pearl" in here?
Follow my mother!   (KING *dies*)

LAERTES

               He is justly served;
It is a poison tempered by himself.
Exchange forgiveness with me, noble Hamlet;
Mine and my father's death come not upon you,
Nor yours on me!   (*Dies*)

HAMLET

Heaven make you free of it! I follow you.—
I am dead, Horatio.—Wretched queen, adieu!—
You that look pale and tremble at this chance,
That are but mutes or audience to this act,
Had I but time—as this fell sergeant, Death,
Is strict in his arrest—O, I could tell you. . . .
But let it be.—Horatio, I am dead;
You live; report me and my cause aright
To the unsatisfied.

HORATIO

                      Never believe it;
I am more an antique Roman than a Dane;
Here's yet some liquor left. (*Seizes the poisoned cup*)

HAMLET

                       As you're a man,
Give me the cup; let go, by heaven, I'll have it!
    (*Knocks the cup out of* HORATIO's *hand*)
O God! Horatio, what a wounded name,
Things standing thus unknown, shall live behind me!
If you did ever hold me in your heart,
Absent you from felicity awhile,
And in this harsh world draw your breath in pain,
To tell my story.
    (*March afar off, and shot O.S.*)
        (*Enters a* GUARD, *and reports softly to* OSRIC)
               What warlike noise is this?

OSRIC

Young Fortinbras, with conquest come from Poland,
To the ambassadors of England gives
This warlike volley.

HAMLET

                    Oh, I die, Horatio;
The potent poison quite o'ercomes my spirit.
I cannot live to hear the news from England,
But I do prophesy the election lights
On Fortinbras; he has my dying voice.
So tell him, with the occurrences, great and small,
Which have brought this about. The rest is silence.

                                           (*Dies*)

HORATIO

Now cracks a noble heart. Good night, sweet prince,
And flights of angels sing you to your rest!
      (*March O.S.—Enter* FORTINBRAS, *the* ENGLISH AMBAS-
      SADORS, *with drums, colours, and* ATTENDANTS)

FORTINBRAS

Where is this sight?

HORATIO

                    What is it you would see?
If aught of woe or wonder, cease your search.

FORTINBRAS

These bodies cry of havoc! Oh, proud Death,
What feast is toward in your eternal cell,
That you so many princes at a shot
So bloodily have struck!

AMBASSADOR

                      The sight is dismal.

HORATIO

Since so precisely on this bloody moment,
You from the Polack wars, and you from England,

Are here arrived, give order that these bodies
High on a stage be placed for viewing;
And let me speak to the yet unknowing world
How these things came about.

     (*Takes out of his doublet the* KING'S *"commission,"*
     which HAMLET *has given him:*)

                         So shall you hear
Of carnal, bloody, and unnatural acts,
Of accidental judgements, casual slaughters,
Of deaths put on by cunning and forced cause,
And, in this upshot, purposes mistook
Fallen on the inventors' heads. All this can I
Truly deliver.

FORTINBRAS

         Let us haste to hear it;
And call the noblest to the audience.
For me, with sorrow I embrace my fortune.
I have some rights of memory in this kingdom,
Which now to claim my vantage does invite me.

HORATIO

Of that I shall have also cause to speak,
And from his mouth whose voice will draw on more.
But let this be immediately performed,
Even while men's minds are wild, lest more mischance
From plots and errors happen.

FORTINBRAS

               Let four captains
Bear Hamlet, like a soldier, to the stage;
For he was likely, had he been put on,
To have proved most royal; and, for his passage,

The soldiers' music and the rites of war
Speak loudly for him.
Go, bid the soldiers shoot.

(*A dead march. Exeunt—four* CAPTAINS *bearing off the
body of* HAMLET. *A peal of ordnance is shot O.S.*)